G000162484

A Matter of Self-confidence - Part I
An introduction to self-confidence coaching in a book

Also by Elizabeth J Tucker:

Simply Stress (Stress Management Exercises, Strategies and Techniques)

The 7 Deadly Sins of Chairing Meetings (Let's Get it Right Every Time)

The 5 P's For a Perfect Meeting (A Step-by-step Guide to Navigate Meetings Like a Pro)

Success Starts Here (Things Every Minute Taker Should Know)

Books by Eliza-Jane Jackson:

Why Doesn't The Law Of Attraction Work?

Creating Prosperity and Abundance

Create Your Own Prosperity Wheel (A step-by-step guide to using The Law of Attraction to manifest the things you want!)

Publisher: Shepherd Creative Learning

Publisher's Note:

The author has made every reasonable attempt to achieve complete accuracy of the content in this book prior to going to press. The publisher, the editor and the author cannot accept responsibility for any errors or omissions, however caused.

You should use this information as you see fit, and at your own risk. You should adjust your use of this information and recommendations accordingly.

Finally, use your own wisdom as guidance. Nothing in this book is intended to replace common sense, legal, or other professional advice. This book is meant to inform and entertain the reader.

No responsibility for loss or damage occasioned to any person acting, or refraining from action, as a result of the material in this publication can be accepted by the publisher, the author or the editor.

A Matter of Self-confidence - Part I
An introduction to self-confidence coaching in a book

Author: Elizabeth J Tucker

Publisher: Shepherd Creative Learning
Year of Publication: 2015

Copyright:

First published in 2015

Apart from any fair dealing for the purposes of research or private study, or criticism or review, as permitted under the Copyright, Designs and Patents Act 1988, this publication may only be reproduced, stored or transmitted in any form or by any means, with the prior permission in writing of the publisher, or in the case of reprographic reproduction in accordance with the terms and licences issued by the CLA.

© Elizabeth J Tucker 2015

The right of Elizabeth J Tucker to be identified as the author of this work has been asserted by her in accordance with the Copyright, Designs and Patents Act 1988.

First Printing: 2015

ISBN: 978-0-9931145-1-9

Publisher: Shepherd Creative Learning

(www.shepherdcreativelearning.co.uk)

Book cover designed by Tristan King - V o o d o o   D e s i g n (www.voodoodesignshropshire.com)

Copyright © Elizabeth J Tucker 2015

Dedication:

The book is dedicated to Dennis Shepherd, Rosemary and Geoffrey Tucker and Richard and Minna Jackson. Huge thanks to you all.

Thanks also to Hugh Price (my funny, inspiring and supportive cousin). 'A Matter of Self-confidence' is the result of one of our deep and meaningful kitchen table conversations.

This book is also dedicated to all the people who have contributed case studies, tried the exercises in this book before going to press or been responsible for the proofreading. Thank you for sharing your views, experiences and questions to help make this book possible.

About the Author:

Elizabeth lives in the heart of the Warwickshire countryside - a place for creative thinking, and a relaxing space for friends and clients to find themselves.

Elizabeth spent many years working in the corporate world, but in 2003 opportunity knocked on her door. She was offered redundancy, which proved to be her launchpad for a whole new career.

In 2003 Elizabeth launched her own, successful, business consultancy. Since then she has had the privilege of working with a diverse client base. Her clients have included The Chartered Institute of Housing, blue chip companies, the British Army, charities, social housing providers, SME and start-up businesses, and personal clients.

Aside from running her own consultancy business, Elizabeth is a writer, intuitive life coach and holistic therapist.

She describes herself as an enthusiastic go-getter with a passion for helping others achieve their goals. Elizabeth uses her own unique blend of insight, wisdom and humour in her work. Her catchphrase is "I will believe in you even when you don't".

Elizabeth is an innovative presenter with an engaging manner. She has spent years helping people overcome their lack of self-confidence and turn aspirations into achievements.

As an author, Elizabeth writes her books based on her experience and knowledge. She believes passionately in the benefits of sharing skills and knowledge to help others create their own success stories.

"It's a privilege to provide support and encouragement to my clients. It's a humbling experience to watch clients break out of their restrictive cocoon and blossom into beautiful butterflies. My mum gave me the wings to fly; now that's what I'm doing for others".

If you would like to know more about Elizabeth or get in touch, you will find her on LinkedIn, Facebook and Twitter. LinkedIn profile (liz-tucker/10/531/68/), Twitter - @liztucker03. Alternatively you can get in touch by email - shepherdcreativelearning@gmail.com

Table of Contents

Preface:

I would like everyone to realise that self-confidence is not an impossible dream; it's available to all of us. What's more, self-confidence doesn't recognise status, race, financial wealth or anything else that we use to define ourselves.

Wouldn't it be lovely if everyone could demonstrate self-confidence all the time. Of course this isn't going to happen for a multitude of reasons. Some people won't have the desire or motivation. Others may not have the support network or the funds to pay for professional help. Some may even believe it's not an option available to them.

Obviously professional help and support is the ideal solution. This option provides you with all the support and encouragement you need to succeed. Not everyone wants or can afford this option.

I believe doing nothing is not a good choice. That's why I chose to write a self-confidence home study programme and a self-help book. If you would like to know more about our home study programmes please look at our website - www.shepherdcreativelearning.co.uk. Alternatively, you can email shepherdcreativelearning@gmail.com.

'A Matter of Self-confidence - Part I' is an easy to read and practical self-help book. Within these pages you will find a combination of subject matter, exercises, inspirational quotes and real life case studies.

My aim in writing this book is to help you regain some of the faith in yourself that you've lost. I'm not suggesting 'A Matter of Self-confidence' will fix all your self-confidence issues. However, it's designed to help you on your journey to a new, more confident you. As your self-confidence grows I'm sure you'll be motivated to keep going.

There are lots of books available on transactional analysis, neuro linguistic programming (NLP) and psychology, which include self-confidence. Most of these books are written from a technical or clinical perspective. This book is written from a different professional perspective.

'A Matter of Self-confidence' is written from the perspective of an intuitive life coach. It's based on my personal experiences and what my clients have experienced. For some clients their aspirations are business or professional goals. For some it's personal, but for many their goal is greater self-confidence.

It's a humbling experience to watch your clients self-confidence develop and see them blossom. It's rather like being a parent; knowing you've equipped your children with the survival skills they need for life.

I've had my share of confidence ups and downs, but that's life. I've chosen to fight back and win. The thing is I've experienced what you're experiencing. In short, I've walked the walk. This is not a theoretical book; it's a practical one based on experience (mine and others).

I realised I would waste a lot of my life if I waited for someone else's permission to be confident. That was the kick in the pants that put me on my journey to self-confidence, and I've never looked back since. I'm still travelling but the journey is easier and more enjoyable these days.

In 2013 I had a lightbulb moment. I realised that more and more clients were asking for self-confidence coaching. Suddenly the seed was sown for a self-confidence home study programme and a self-help book.

In 2013 I spent the majority of my time helping clients improve their self-confidence. In the spring of 2014 'A Matter of Self-confidence' was born and started to grow organically. From this point onwards I started to pull together my skills, knowledge, experience and observations.

Here we are in 2015 - 'A Matter of Self-confidence - (Parts I and II)' are ready to reach out and help you increase your self-confidence. I hope this small investment will open the door to new self-confidence and new opportunities for you.

Self-confidence - everyone can have it but not everyone knows how to achieve it. That's my job! If you don't know how to achieve your desired level of self-confidence, find the help you need. This could be a professional life coach, home study programme, self-help book like this one or your own support network. There are lots of options available.

Self-confidence is one of the best gifts you can ever give yourself. You won't regret it.

"No matter how great or small your fears are - it takes an equal amount of bravery to conquer them. Don't let fear hold you back and stop you being confident" - Elizabeth J Tucker

1. Introduction

"Confidence is a magnet to success" - E'yen A Gardner

Everyone experiences a lack of self-confidence at some point; no matter how successful they are. Lack of self-confidence can be a temporary blip, long-term or even debilitating. Everyone's experience of self-confidence, or lack of it, is different.

Everywhere you look there are myths. Self-confidence is no different. Have you grown up believing that self-confidence is something you have or don't have? Let's dispel this myth straightaway. We all have confidence in certain aspects of our life. What's more with effort and commitment you can develop self-confidence in other areas of your life too.

While we're on the subject of myths, here are three more:

1. You have to be born with it
Wrong! Self-confidence is a skill that can be learned. It's just like learning to walk, drive, play a game or anything else you've learnt to do

2. If your self-confidence has been destroyed it's gone for good
Wrong! It may take a greater leap of faith to start building your self-confidence back up, but it can be done. You have to want your self-confidence back though. Some people prefer to be a victim

3. I'll know I'm confident when I can be sure I'll succeed at something new
Wrong! How can you know you'll succeed when you've never done something before? Fear of failure is what's blocking your self-confidence

No matter how confident you are there will always be times in your life when your self-confidence takes a knock. A crisis of confidence can creep up on you slowly or hit you hard and fast like an electric shock.

Do you have a strategy for recovering from a crisis of confidence? If not, ask yourself "If this was happening to a friend, what advice would I give him/her?" Nurturing at this early stage can stop your lack of self-confidence spiralling downwards.

Here is an opportunity to reflect on a crisis of confidence that you've experienced at some point in your life.

Exercise: Crisis of Confidence

Think of a situation that resulted in you having a crisis of confidence. Try to remember this in as much detail as possible (even if it's painful to do so). All you need for this exercise is a piece of paper and a pen. When you're ready answer the following questions:

1. What was the experience that caused you a crisis of confidence? Write this memory in as much detail as you can remember

2. Did this creep up on you slowly, or was it quick and unexpected?

3. Did you get over this crisis of confidence or is it still holding you back in some way?

4. How long did it take to get over this experience?

5. How did you overcome this crisis of confidence?

6. Did you give yourself a pat on the back after you had overcome this challenge? Or, did you just get on with the next thing that needed dealing with?

7. How did you feel afterwards? Did you go back to being the same person you were before, or did it change you in some way?

8. What emotions has this exercise stirred up in you? Are you able to release these emotions or do you need some help? If you need some help, seek professional help or talk to someone in your support network

9. What have you learnt about yourself from this exercise?

"Develop a rock solid faith in yourself. Know that you're great as you are. Just ask your friends" - Elizabeth J Tucker

I've had my share of confidence ups and downs. My confidence issues started as a young child. Some disappeared quickly but others hung around well into adulthood.

Fear of change and fear of failure were often the reason I failed to reach my full potential. I didn't have the self-confidence to dip my toe in the water. For many years I didn't have the self-confidence to face my fears. The end result was a lot of wasted years in the lack of self-confidence desert.

I kept asking "How do I overcome my fears and lack of self-confidence?" I didn't know the answer at the time, but I had the tenacity to keep searching. Then I learnt that repetition is the mother of all skills. Repetitive messages have the power to build or destroy your self-confidence.

From this I learnt to change the message. I realise that's a very simplistic explanation. Of course it wasn't quite as simple as that, but that in essence is what happened.

I still lack self-confidence on occasions, but now I know that I can overcome my challenges. No matter what, I know that I will come out the other side. I've done this lots of times now and each success provides the motivation for greater success.

My advice is just be who you are and accept this unconditionally. Pretending to be someone you're not is exhausting and will never bring you true happiness. By accepting yourself as you are you will always present the best you. Remember, your friends like 'you', not who you aspire to be.

Most of us are kinder to other people than we are to ourselves. Does this describe you? When something major happens in your life treat yourself more gently than usual. Treat yourself as you would one of your friends if they were in crisis.

Constantly making negative comments about yourself is not an endearing characteristic. It will put people off wanting to be around you. There are two possible messages this habit sends out to other people. It suggests you either lack self-confidence or you're attention seeking using reverse psychology. Either way, it's not a winning formula.

Neither of these messages will make people warm to you. Furthermore, this thinking may create feelings of isolation. Feelings of isolation have the potential to further harm your self-esteem or self-confidence. Don't put yourself through this needlessly.

In the Appendices section (Chapter 10) I have included a 12-week self-confidence plotter. You may like to use this to monitor your progress from today until the end of week 12. I'm sure you will identify a positive shift in your self-confidence level. Hopefully this will inspire you to keep working towards the goal of greater self-confidence.

'A Matter of Self-confidence' is written from the perspective of an intuitive life coach. It includes my findings from working with my clients, exercises, pearls of wisdom and case studies. The case studies are from real people who have kindly given me permission to share their story. The exercises will give you an opportunity to reflect, take stock or take a deeper look at yourself.

I'm sure you have preconceived ideas about self-confidence. We all do. Do you already know what your preconceived ideas are? If not, here's a quick quiz to help you identify your self-confidence beliefs.

Exercise: Reality or Myth Quiz

The thing about assumptions is sometimes they are correct, but equally they could be totally wrong. Try this short quiz and see if you can identify what is a self-confidence reality and what is myth.

1. We are all born confident - Reality/Myth

2. I had a difficult or emotionally barren childhood. As a result of this I will never be confident - Reality/Myth

3. I know I lack self-confidence as I'm nervous in social situations - Reality/Myth

4. I lack self-confidence as I'm not as attractive or smart as the other people in my network - Reality/Myth

5. Other people keep putting me down, and so I lack self-confidence - Reality/Myth

6. Low self-esteem causes fear - Reality/Myth

7. People with high self-esteem are arrogant - Reality/Myth

8. Everyone can develop self-confidence - Reality/Myth

9. Highly self-confident people also have fears, anxieties and lack of self-confidence sometimes - Reality/Myth

10. Lack of self-confidence comes from our insecurities - Reality/Myth

11. Arrogance and self-confidence is the same thing - Reality/Myth

You will find the answers to this quiz in the appendices section at the end of the book.

As I've previously stated, self-confidence is available to everyone who welcomes it. In order to make self-confidence your reality you need:

- A genuine desire to achieve self-confidence

- A commitment to put in the time and effort. Remember, wanting and achieving are very different things

- A good support network

- Some short, medium and long-term goals. These need to be stretching but achievable

- Some exercises to test how you're doing

- A willingness to look inside yourself and take the time to really understand yourself. This may be uncomfortable at times

- A self-belief that you can achieve your goals, and you're worth it!

- Rewards for each success

- An open mind

- A willingness to enjoy the process of developing self-confidence

- Gratitude for all the amazing opportunities and experiences life gives you

- To expect a happier and healthier you at the end of the process

One thing I've learnt from my own self-confidence journey is it could have been easier. The process didn't need to be as slow or painful as I made it. I wish I'd found the answers sooner.

"Just because you're from a small town doesn't mean that you're small. Don't ever think anyone's more important than you are, or has more valid experiences" - Gwendolyn Heasley

I hope you find some useful nuggets in 'A Matter of Self-confidence'. Self-confidence is an internal state and only you can do something about it. Thank you for allowing me to play a small part in your journey to self-confidence.

Some chapters of this book will be more relevant to you than others. You can either read the book cover to cover or just dip into the chapters that you feel are relevant at this time. There is no right or wrong way to face up to your self-confidence issues. Doing nothing is the only wrong choice.

If you would like to share your self-confidence story or observations please do get in touch - shepherdcreativelearning@gmail.com.

"Confidence is not a wilted plant that can be brought back to life with a bit of water. It's a highly flammable object. Doubt sets it aflame and destroys it irreparably" - Michèle Halberstadt

2. What is Self-confidence?

"Self-confidence is a belief in your ability to succeed. Lack of self-confidence stops you even trying. Don't let lack of self-confidence hold you back" - Elizabeth J Tucker

What is self-confidence? It's that elusive thing that some people seem to have in spades, while others have none. Until you understand what self-confidence is you can't tackle your issues or enjoy the benefits of it.

Do you believe that self-confidence is external? It's not. Self-confidence sits inside you, not outside of you. How often have you heard someone say "I don't have any self-confidence"? The suggestion is this is some mysterious thing that hasn't been given to them yet.

The internal emotions you experience govern the quality of your life. The emotional state of self-confidence touches every aspect of your life, and only you can control it. It's essential to recognise this; otherwise you will always be looking for the solution in your external environment.

Although self-confidence is an emotional state that can only be felt internally your subsequent behaviour will be external. Far too much time is wasted by people believing they will be confident when something external happens. This could be losing weight or becoming a subject matter expert. Others believe they will become confident when they achieve a promotion or gain additional qualifications.

All of these assumptions are wrong. We all have self-confidence and insecurities, in varying degrees. The good news is suffering from lack of self-confidence is not mandatory. You can choose to spend the rest of your life lacking self-confidence or embrace change. Which will you choose?

True self-confidence is a happy and comfortable emotional state of being. Self-confidence is something you will feel sometimes and not at other times. It's like a good friendship; something to be valued and nurtured. Self-confidence is also:

- Liberating
- Empowering
- Sexy
- Available to everyone
- A choice each of us makes for ourselves

- Gives us the courage to overcome our fears
- The best gift we can ever give ourselves

Self-confidence doesn't rely on putting others down, or measuring yourself against anyone else. When you're genuinely confident you have a healthy respect for yourself and others. Knowing this, who wouldn't want to make room for self-confidence in their life?

Of course it's possible to be overconfident, or appear overconfident. People who give the impression of overconfidence often appear arrogant or cocky. This may just be a front though. The reality is often a lack of self-confidence, which is masked as overconfidence.

The Self-Esteem Institute claims that those who lack self-confidence expect failure, which may lead to the extremes of overachieving or underachieving. Historically I've been guilty of driving myself to overachieving to conceal my lack of self-confidence. These days, I have a more sensible head on my shoulders.

Self-confidence is how you view your abilities and will vary from situation to situation. It's about knowing what you're good at and the value you provide. It's also acting in a way that conveys this message to others.

When you reach a state of true self-confidence you will succeed because of your ability. This is quite different to the ability to talk about what you're good at. Genuinely confident people are aware of their strengths and weaknesses, and accept both graciously.

When you experience genuine self-confidence you don't always need to tell others about your abilities. Of course we all like sincere praise, like being told you're good at something. We are all human after all.

How confident are you? Everyone has a level of self-confidence in some area of his/her life. For each of us this will be different, so don't compare yourself to other people. Do you have any of the following skills?

- Drive (car, lorry or bus)
- Have a job
- Train or teach other people at work, in a school, college or university
- Have a family
- Dance (for fun or professionally)
- Play sport (for fun or competitively)
- Play a musical instrument

- Are you a member of a club?

If you answered yes to any of these then pat yourself on the back. Each of these skills requires a degree of self-confidence. You had to learn these skills, and doing so increased your self-confidence in this area.

You might like to consider all the areas of your life. By identifying where you're confident and where you lack self-confidence you can decide what action to take.

Exercise: What Does Self-confidence Mean To Me?

The first step to building self-confidence is assessing what self-confidence means to you personally. Just saying "I want to be more confident" isn't going to fix anything as it's too vague to be useful.

The only resources you need for this short exercise are a piece of paper and a pen.

1. On a sheet of paper write or draw what self-confidence means to you. For example, "when I'm with a new group of people I want to feel relaxed and join in the conversation". If you prefer to draw a picture, your images need to convey what self-confidence looks like to you

2. If you choose to write your answers (rather than draw a picture) start each sentence with one of the following:

"I want to be able to..."
"I want to do...."
"I want to be..."

Each statement needs to be positive. Don't write 'I don't want', avoiding statements or any other negative messages

3. In which situations or parts of your life do you need more self-confidence? Don't just write the word 'everything'. The only way to improve your self-confidence is to honestly appraise your life and your current confidence level

4. In which situations or parts of your life are you already confident? For example - I'm a good cook, excellent with numbers or accounts, gardening, working with children, being a great parent, driving etc. Be honest with yourself but don't be too modest

5. Look at your responses to question 4. Spend a few minutes savouring in your achievements to date. Feel proud of all the things you can already

do confidently. If you've never done this before it may feel alien but stick with it

6. Now write down one area of your life where you would like greater self-confidence. For example perhaps your answer is career/work. You probably want greater self-confidence in several areas of your life but you can't tackle them all at once

7. Write or draw one thing you will be able to do once you have the self-confidence you desire in this area. This should be something tangible like apply for a job, deal with a challenging person or situation, public speaking etc

8. You have now given yourself a goal to work towards. How long are you going to give yourself to achieve this goal?

9. How will you reward yourself when you achieve this goal? It's important to reward every success. Recognising achievements is an important strategy in developing self-confidence

The terms self-confidence and self-esteem are often confused. There is a subtle but important difference. It's helpful to understand the difference when looking to improve your overall sense of self as one feeds the other.

Self-esteem is your opinion of your self-worth or personal value. It's also about whether you believe you're worthy of respect from others. We all develop self-esteem from our life experiences and situations. These are the things that have shaped how you view yourself.

Self-confidence is how you feel about your abilities and can vary from situation to situation. Your self-confidence will vary for each different area of your life.

You may have a healthy self-esteem, but low self-confidence in certain areas of your life or in certain situations. Perhaps you're the life and soul of the party when you're with friends but have no self-confidence in business meetings. Public speaking might scare you to death while sharing your knowledge one-to-one is easy to do. The possibilities are endless.

"In order to improve your self-esteem you first need to truly like yourself. Start by trying to see the person your friends see" - Elizabeth J Tucker

When you love yourself (in a healthy way) your self-esteem improves and you become more self-confident. When you feel confident you begin to increase your overall sense of self-esteem. It's a continuous cycle. Ideally you want to have a good sense of self-esteem and self-confidence. This is achievable but it takes time and effort.

Low self-esteem comes from a poor self-image. Too little self-esteem can leave you feeling defeated or depressed. It often leads people to make poor decisions. This frequently includes destructive relationships.

Do you think you're a good, reliable, hardworking, honest or friendly person? Do you like what you see when you look in the mirror? Or, do you believe others look better, dress better than you, or are more capable than you? Here's an exercise to help you identify your perception of your self-esteem.

Exercise: My Self-esteem Checklist

This exercise is an opportunity for you to do a little self-reflection. The answers will help you to form a clear picture of your overall perception of yourself.

Don't spend too long answering each question. Trust your instinct and take the first answer that pops into your head.

The only resources you need for this short exercise are a piece of paper and a pen.

1. Answer each question with - Yes/No/Sometimes/Usually. Don't be tempted to write an explanation or justify your answers

a. My experiences in life have taught me to value and appreciate myself

b. I have learnt not to be judgemental of myself and other people

c. I believe that only I can make me feel good about myself

d. I like myself and enjoy my own company

e. I easily acknowledge my skills, strengths and assets, and I pat myself on the back when I do something well

f. I generally feel good about myself

g. I feel I am entitled to other people's attention, time, friendship and love

h. I have learnt to lessen my expectations of myself. My expectations of me are no longer rigid or harsh. I treat myself in the same way as I treat other people

i. I am kind and encouraging towards myself, rather than self-critical

j. My inner talk is comforting and helpful. When I make a mistake I'm kind to myself and encourage myself to move on quickly

k. I think I deserve to treat myself to nice things and think that I'm worthy of a great life

l. I understand why people like me and enjoy my company

2. Look at your answers and identify whether they were mostly 'Yes, No, Sometimes or Usually'. Now read the analysis below

Analysis:

Mostly yes - You have a healthy view of your self-worth. This is excellent news; just make sure it's genuine self-confidence and not inflated ego. Don't get complacent as maintaining self-confidence is a continuous and lifelong process

Mostly usually - On the whole you have a healthy view of your self-worth. Were you just being modest when you answered these questions? What will it take to move you to yes?

Mostly sometimes - Your self-perception seems to be patchy – sometimes good and sometimes bad. Look at the questions where you answered sometimes. Identify what you can do to change this to 'usually' or even 'yes'

Mostly no - Oh dear, you don't have a very high opinion of yourself do you. Your journey to self-confidence may seem like hard work initially but the rewards will be worth it. Remember you deserve to be happy, healthy and confident. I hope you stick with it

Arrogance is sometimes confused with self-confidence, although they are not the same thing at all. Arrogant people demonstrate some easily identifiable traits, which can be summarised as an exaggeration of their ability. Here are some typical traits of arrogance:

- An inflated idea of your own ability, coupled with a desire to look down on others
- Thinking less of others (either their ability or views/opinions)
- Correcting other people's flaws
- Needing to show others the right way to do things (whether they want to be shown or not)
- Going all out to prove you're right
- Being right is more important than being capable

It's worth remembering that arrogance is often a smokescreen for lack of self-confidence or lack of self-esteem. If you're on the receiving end of arrogance it can be difficult to demonstrate tolerance and understanding though.

Narcissism is not the same as self-confidence, self-esteem or even arrogance. Narcissism is about the ego, and believing that you're the centre of the universe. Freud named Narcissism after the mythological figure of Narcissus.

In case you don't know the story of Narcissus... Echo was a wood nymph who loved a youth by the name of Narcissus. Narcissus was a beautiful creature loved by many but Narcissus loved no one in return. He enjoyed attention, praise and envy. In Narcissus' eyes nobody matched him. He considered none were worthy of him.

One day whilst out enjoying the sunshine Narcissus came upon a pool of water. As he gazed into it he caught a glimpse of what he thought was a beautiful water spirit. He did not recognise his own reflection and was immediately enamoured. Narcissus bent down his head to kiss the vision.

As he did so the reflection mimicked his actions. Taking this as a sign of reciprocation Narcissus reached into the pool to draw the water spirit to him. The water displaced and the vision was gone. He panicked, where had his love gone?

When the water became calm the water spirit returned. "Why, beautiful being, do you shun me? Surely my face is not one to repel you. The nymphs love me, and you yourself look not indifferent upon me. When I stretch forth my arms you do the same; and you smile upon me and answer my beckoning with the like".

Again he reached out and again his love disappeared. Frightened to touch the water Narcissus lay still by the pool gazing in to the eyes of his vision. He did not move, he did not eat or drink, he only suffered.

As he pined he became gaunt losing his beauty. The nymphs that loved him pleaded with him to come away from the pool. He was transfixed; he wanted to stay there forever. Narcissus died as a result of his grief.

As humans we all enjoy occasional admiration. This doesn't make us narcissists though. What separates narcissists from the rest of us is their constant desire for admiration.

Narcissism is basically a psychological coping mechanism for low self-esteem. Ironically the narcissist rarely believes that he/she has a problem with self-esteem. Don't get hung up on this as most of us are not narcissists.

How you see the world affects your emotional state and vice-versa. Therefore, it's helpful to recognise your default position. Is your default position positive or negative? If you don't already know the answer, try this exercise and find out.

Exercise: My Default Position

As I've just said, how you see the world affects your emotional state. You don't need any resources for this exercise; it's simply requires a few moments of reflection. Stop for a moment and consider the following:

1. Think of someone you know whose default is always negative. Choose just one person to focus on (even though you can probably think of several)

2. Now think of someone you know who always appears to have a positive view of life no matter what's occurring

3. For both people, consider their attitude, tone of voice, body language and choice of words

4. Which one are you most comfortable being with? How do you feel when you're in this person's company?

5. Now think about yourself. Which of these people are you most like? Be honest with yourself. What characteristics do you share with this person?

6. Is your default position positive or negative? Were you surprised to discover your default position?

7. Now read the analysis below and decide what, if anything, you're going to do about it

Analysis:

Positive - This is a good start. If your default position is positive you will probably find the journey to sustainable self-confidence easier. Decide which areas of your life need a confidence boost and why

Negative - If you constantly live in a negative state your journey to self-confidence may feel like you're walking through treacle. If you identified that your default position is 'negative', ask yourself what you're willing to do about it. If you do nothing about it you will continue to be plagued by negative thinking and lack of self-confidence

Was your default position positive or negative? Were you conscious of your default position before you did this exercise? Obviously positive thinking alone is not enough, but it does have a part to play in developing self-confidence. If nothing else, I challenge you to try to adopt a more positive mindset.

Just to recap... here are some facts about self-confidence:

- Genuinely confident people recognise that they can't control everything and accept they have limited abilities in some areas. They don't allow this to hold them back though

- If you don't break out of your lack of self-confidence bubble nothing will ever change

- Only you can change your lack of self-confidence. You may not want to hear this but perhaps you're in a comfortable negative rut. I know this can be uncomfortable to acknowledge but denial isn't going to help you

- Confident people have a healthy respect for their abilities. They don't have a constant down on themselves or anyone else

- Yes, you can be confident! Just dare to dream and believe. You have to be willing to work at it. Self-confidence doesn't happen without effort and practice

- Your past doesn't have to control your future. Every little bit of self-confidence you develop will make you feel more positive

- If you surround yourself with positive people they will rub off on you. Before you know it, your own self-belief system will develop and you will be influencing others

- You may need to develop some mental toughness. Don't take every rejection or negative comment personally

- Nothing increases self-confidence like overcoming your fears. Do things that scare you and then reward your successes

- Good verbal and non-verbal communication skills are useful in every area of your life. Nothing is wasted. Everything you learn will add to your self-confidence toolkit

- You are responsible for your own lack of self-confidence. Others may fire the bullets and arrows but you choose to allow them to wound you

Do yourself a favour and say 'No' to lack of self-confidence. Remember, you're worth it!

Self-confidence is a wonderful feeling, and offers many benefits. I wrote 'A Matter of Self-confidence' as a self-help tool as I want as many people as possible to enjoy self-confidence. I hope it will help increase your level of self-confidence in some way.

The sky's the limit; you will decide when to stop building your self-confidence. I hope you feel empowered by this statement. Your imagination is a powerful tool. Don't let your mind control you and keep you in a negative state. Instead stride out and be the beautiful and confident soul you're meant to be.

"Self-confidence - that's what makes people beautiful" - Elizabeth J Tucker

3. Get To Know Yourself

"Too many people overvalue what they are not and undervalue what they are" - Malcolm S Forbes

Malcolm Forbes words are so true. Think about them for a moment. How well do you really know yourself? Do you truly value what and who you are? If you lack self-confidence the answer is probably no.

No one can ever know you as completely as you know yourself. Others may think they know you, but their judgement is based on how you project yourself. Only you know everything that is going on in your head.

In order to increase your self-confidence you first need to truly understand yourself. This involves an awareness of your current confidence level and how life's slings and arrows got you to this point. You didn't just wake up one day saying "I think I'll allow lack of self-confidence to rule my life". Your lack of self-confidence is probably due to a range of experiences.

Next you need to ask yourself "do I want to change?" After this you need to decide that you're going to change. Finally, it's about the commitment to succeed. Without a genuine commitment to change you're wasting your time.

Before moving on ask yourself "do I want to change?" Spend a few minutes reflecting on this. Your instant answer is probably yes of course I do; I don't want to feel like this forever. Dig a little deeper. Do you really want to change? Are you prepared to embrace change?

For a lot of people change is scary. It requires a leap of faith and stepping into the unknown. Not everyone feels comfortable with change. You will find more about change in chapter 8 - Change, Fear and Self-confidence.

The next question to ask yourself is "Am I ready to change?" Change can be uncomfortable as it will take you out of the rut you're in. Every cycle of change involves some discomfort or pain before you can enjoy the benefits.

If you decide that you are ready to challenge yourself to be more confident your journey has now begun. On a scale of zero to ten how committed are you to achieving this goal? Don't make an unrealistic promise to yourself as failing to live up to your expectations will simply set you back.

The final question to ask yourself at this point is - "how will I reward myself?" It's important to have a reward at the end of your achievement. Rewards help provide the motivation to keep going.

You may not notice your self-confidence growing as the changes can be subtle and minimal initially. Sometimes you may cancel out your progress by allowing negative thoughts to run riot in your head. You may even brush aside or simply ignore the signs as you're busy focusing on the next goal.

One day something will stop you in your tracks. It will make you stop and really look at yourself. This might be the first time you realise how your self-confidence has grown. Hopefully this will be an exciting discovery for you.

In order to be able to recognise how much your self-confidence is growing you need to know what your starting point is. This exercise is designed to help you identify your self-confidence starting point.

"Self-confidence is an interesting thing. As you get older your self-confidence comes from knowing who you are rather than how you look" - Elizabeth J Tucker

Exercise: My Current Confidence Level

The more aware you become of your growing self-confidence the more confident you will become, and so it goes on. You may like to repeat this exercise each time you face a big challenge in your life. If so, identify your self-confidence level before and after you've dealt with your major issue/challenge.

The only resources you need for this short exercise are a piece of paper and a pen. There are just four steps to this exercise:

1. On a piece of paper create an 'L' shaped chart like the example below. Along the bottom of your chart write the numbers 0 - 10 (space the numbers out evenly).

Next, place evenly spaced markers up the left hand side of your chart. You can have as many or as few markers as you like. At the first marker put today's date. Each time you do this exercise in future put the date against the next marker

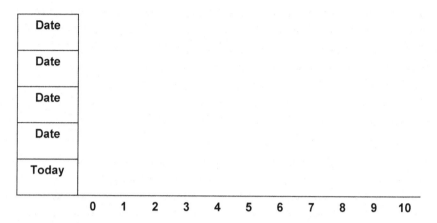

Date	
Date	
Date	
Date	
Today	

0   1   2   3   4   5   6   7   8   9   10

2. Put a cross in the place that represents your current self-confidence level. 0 = no self-confidence and 10 = very confident (not cocky or arrogant, just confident). Don't dwell on it; just place the cross where you instinctively feel is the right place. For example you may decide your confidence level is 4 today

3. Wherever you have placed your cross (e.g. 4) imagine how you would feel if your score moved up just one place (e.g. 4 - 5). What would be different? How would this progress make you feel? Now you have a goal to work towards (you're working to the next level on the confidence scale)

4. Each time you face a challenging situation, where you lack self-confidence, make a note of your confidence level before you tackle the issue. Then record your score after you've dealt with the issue. It's important to recognise and reward each success

Note: There is a chance that your confidence level won't increase, but generally every challenge will improve your self-confidence. Don't expect this to be a major leap each time.

Every time you tackle a situation that takes you outside your comfort zone you grow a little. From every experience you will learn something. This may be new skills, self-confidence or even resilience. No experience is ever wasted.

"Just like when spring comes, before the first green shoots appear, things are happening beneath the surface" - Elizabeth J Tucker

Now you know where you are on the self-confidence scale are you ready to do something about it? Do you genuinely want to increase your self-confidence? If so, how will you benefit from greater self-confidence? Answer these four questions:

1. In which aspects of your life are you happy with your current confidence level?

2. Think about the positive feelings you experience when you're feeling confident. How do you feel, or what do you experience? What is it that tells you you're feeling confident?

3. Now think about where you lack self-confidence. What are the emotions you experience when you lack self-confidence?

4. Now compare your answers to question 2 and 3. What's different?

The more in tune you are with yourself the sooner you will notice your self-confidence growing. Learning to be happy and comfortable in your own skin isn't arrogance; it's self-confidence. Being at peace with yourself is a truly amazing experience.

It's important to spend time thinking about who you are now and who you want to be. I'm not suggesting that you undergo a personality transplant. Self-confidence is about enabling you to shine. It's about allowing other people to see the real you instead of the anxious, low self-confidence person you currently are.

Take the time to really get to know yourself. More importantly, learn to like and love the person you are. See the person your friends see.

"We know what we are, but not what we may be" - William Shakespeare

We're all special, so what's special about you? You're unique so that alone makes you special, but I want you to think a little deeper. The next exercise is designed to help you appreciate the person you truly are.

Exercise: What's Special About Me?

If I asked you to write a list of all the things that are special about you how long would your list be? Most people find it easier to talk positively about others. In this exercise you're going to ask other people for their opinion of you. Don't be tempted to bat the compliments away though.

This exercise can be done over a period of days, weeks or months. You can involve as many or as few people as you wish. What's more you can devote as much time to this exercise as you wish.

You will need a journal or notepad to record the feedback from your family, friends and colleagues. You may like to ask yourself the same question and compare your answers to theirs.

1. Decide who you are going to enlist to help you with this exercise. Only choose people whose opinion matters to you

2. Ask each person the same question - "what's special about me?" Don't ask any other questions

3. Make a note of the responses. When you have a few quiet moments, reflect on the lovely feedback you've received from the people who care about you

4. The challenge for you is to believe this feedback. Each time you feel your self-esteem or self-confidence wavering read these positive comments. Learn to believe them as these are sincere observations

"Accept who you are. It's not an over-inflated sense of self-confidence, it's just accepting I am who I am and I'm happy with that" - Elizabeth J Tucker

Before you move on, you might like to reflect on what you have learnt about yourself from this exercise. Most of us learn something that we weren't previously aware of. This may not instantly turn you into a confident person, but it's a good starting point. Do you still agree with the self-confidence level score you gave yourself?

Learning to like, love and value yourself are important building blocks in your wall of self-confidence. Here's a case study that demonstrates we don't really know what we're capable of until we try. This is my own personal story.

Case Study: You don't know what you can do until you try!

I used to be a member of Soroptimist International. If you're interested their website is http://www.soroptimistinternational.org. In 2003 the International Convention was to be held in Sydney. This was an opportunity to be a part of something very special.

Some of the members of my local club were going, so I signed up too. I expected to travel to Sydney with the rest of the group, but eventually everyone went on different dates.

Due to work commitments I was restricted on my outbound travel date. This resulted in me having to travel half way around the world as a lone traveller.

Although I'd been abroad before, I'd never travelled alone short-haul, let alone long-haul. When my tickets arrived I discovered that I had to get connecting flights in Dubai and Singapore. If you've ever been to Dubai Airport you'll know what a scary experience this is.

When I discovered that I would have to travel alone and deal with two connecting flights each way my initial reaction was 'I can't do this'. At this point I seriously considered forfeiting the money and staying at home. Then I thought I can't afford to waste this amount of money. I had saved long and hard for this trip and I had to find the courage to do this.

The journey was long and tiring. Dealing with the connections and transfers did take me out of my comfort zone, but I got through it. I was extremely anxious from the time I left home until I reached my hotel in Sydney. Then I had to repeat the entire exercise to come back home.

The 2003 Soroptimist International convention was an awesome experience. There were approximately 1300 women in Darling Harbour for the convention (imagine all those women in one place!). I met women from all around the world, and had the most amazing time.

I spent time with some of the most confident, powerful and interesting women I have ever encountered. I felt privileged to be rubbing shoulders with them. They made me realise that we're only held back by our own self-limiting beliefs.

When I got back from my amazing trip, I spent some time reflecting on all aspects of the trip. There was so much to reflect on, and I wanted to analyse what I'd learnt. I realised that finding the courage to travel to Sydney alone did wonders for my self-confidence.

This experience taught me that you don't know what you can do until you try it. I also learnt that being far outside your comfort zone won't kill you. I learnt a great deal about myself from this amazing trip. On reflection, I would do it all over again if I had the chance.

(Liz - You don't know what you can do until you try! author)

Are you ready to test your self-confidence again? This is just a short quiz to help you identify how confident you are. You can do this quiz on your own or with a partner. It's supposed to be fun so don't get anxious about it

Exercise: My Self-confidence Quiz

This quick exercise should take no more than 10 minutes. The only resources you need for this exercise are a piece of paper and a pen.

1. Read each question without giving too much thought to your answer. Just choose whichever answer you automatically feel is the right one for you. Answer each question - Yes (Y), No (N), Sometimes (S)

a. Are you comfortable in new situations?

b. Do you do what is expected of you, rather than what you believe is right or want to do?

c. Do you enjoy public speaking or giving a presentation? We all feel nervous, but aside from this we either like or dislike delivering presentations/public speaking

d. When you disagree with someone else's opinion do you make your point calmly and clearly?

e. Do you enjoy new challenges at work?

f. Do you enjoy receiving a new piece of work?

g. Are you embarrassed if you find yourself under or over-dressed for an event?

h. Are you the first on the dance floor at parties?

i. Are you happy to mingle and chat with strangers at parties and social gatherings?

j. Are you comfortable eating alone in restaurants?

k. Are you comfortable walking into a bar or pub to meet friends (even if you're the first to arrive)?

l. Are you anxious before social events?

m. Are you happy to be in a group photograph?

n. Would you feel able to get up and shut the window on a train if you felt cold?

o. If someone jumps in front of you in a queue are you comfortable saying something to them about it?

2. Look at your answers and identify whether they were mostly 'Yes, No or Sometimes'. Now read the analysis below

Analysis:

Mostly yes - You appear to handle most situations confidently. This is a good starting point. Now look at the situations where you feel less confident and make a promise to deal with them

Mostly sometimes - You're on the road to self-confidence but there's clearly more to do. Look at the areas where you feel less confident. What can you do to increase your self-confidence?

Mostly no - You clearly have significant self-confidence issues. Are your self-confidence issues the result of a traumatic event or an accumulation of lifetime events? Clearly it's going to take time and effort to build your self-confidence so decide what you're going to tackle first

Regardless of whether your result was mostly 'yes, sometimes or no', spend a few minutes reflecting. What has this exercise told you about yourself? Next, create a mini action plan. Now you understand yourself better, what three actions are you going to take?

1.

2.

3.

"The more self-confidence you have the better you will deal with life's challenges" - Elizabeth J Tucker

4. The Ego And Self-Confidence

"To walk around with an ego is a bad thing. To have confidence in yourself is a great thing" - Fred Durst

The topic of ego states is massive and can't be covered comprehensively in this book. However, your ego state has a direct link with your self-confidence. This is why I've chosen to briefly touch on the subject.

As I've just said, there is a link between ego and self-confidence. There is also a difference between your ego state and being your true self.

Generally your ego creates feelings of pain, fear and disempowerment. Your ego focuses on past pain and future fears. It also makes you feel needy and anxious, which is unhealthy.

At the other end of the spectrum is narcissism. This is where you're controlled by vanity, conceit or simple selfishness. This is just as unhealthy as being controlled by your ego.

There is a middle ground; that's being your true self. Your true self is sometimes referred to as your natural state of being. It supplies you with feelings of peace, calm, happiness and clarity. Your true self gets you to focus on the now (also known as mindfulness).

By being mindful you take each moment as it comes and are in a better place to be objective about what's occurring in your life. This acceptance helps build self-confidence as you don't practice self-sabotage. Acceptance is also a key factor in successfully managing change.

Do you know if you normally act on ego or are your true self? Try this short quiz to find out.

Exercise: The Difference Between Ego and Your True Self

1. Read each of the following questions and answer them truthfully. Answer each question with Yes, Sometimes or No. It's important to be honest with yourself. Who knows you may be pleasantly surprised

a. Do you need other people to create your happiness?

b. Do you struggle to be the real you when you're around other people?

c. Do you put on a front to try to make other people like you?

d. Do you blame other people and situations when things go wrong?

e. Do you struggle to take responsibility when aspects of your life haven't worked as you wanted them to?

f. Do you struggle to accept other people's opinions and views (particularly if they are negative)?

g. Do you become defensive when confronted with issues or criticism?

h. Do your problems seem to have the same recurring theme?

i. Do you find it difficult to accept other people compliments?

j. Do you have trouble trusting people and situations? Do you expect people to let you down or harm you in some way?

k. Do you often feel the need to be in control?

l. Do you believe your happiness is dependent on what you have?

m. When something negative happens in your life do you think 'why me, or this is typical of my luck'?

n. Are you naturally competitive, feel envious or jealous of other people that may have things you don't?

o. Do you struggle to take responsibility when you make a mistake? Are you immediately looking to place the blame elsewhere?

p. Do you fear being hurt or controlled by the people you love most?

q. Do you believe your ego is a reflection of the real you?

r. Do you constantly feel dissatisfied with your performance? Do you always believe you could have done better?

s. Do you keep revisiting past mistakes in your mind, rather than accepting something has gone wrong and move on?

2. How many of these questions did you respond to with a 'yes'? Add up your score (yes) and read the analysis below

Analysis:

0 - Wow, if you genuinely scored zero, pat yourself on the back. Be an example for others. The world needs people like you!

1 - 4 - This is a very good score. You're human and sometimes you struggle with your ego. Identify where your issues are so you can work on them

5 - 9 - Your score suggests you drift between being your true self and being controlled by your ego. Being judgemental is blocking you from reaching your full potential. Learn to view setbacks as a gift. Setbacks are an opportunity to learn something and grow

10 - 14 - I'm sure you experience some wins in your life, but how long do the memories last? Your life may be a roller-coaster of feeling good then feeling disappointed when life isn't delivering what you believe it should. It's time to release your need to make things happen. Learn to let go of the need to control everything. Also learn to like and love yourself in a healthy way

15 and Over - Oh dear, your ego is ruling your life. You're extremely self-critical and self-judgemental. Your attitude needs to change. It's time to start treating yourself more kindly. If you continue to self-sabotage you will harm whatever self-confidence you have. This will not be a recipe for success

3. Once you've read the analysis decide what, if anything, you're going to do about it. Only you can control the power of your ego, so it's over to you now

The information is this chapter is not detailed, but it will give you an insight into ego states. Hopefully it will help you to be a little more self-aware.

There are three primary ego states. These are parent, adult and child. As you're unique your experience of each ego state will be different to everyone else's.

The 'parent' ego state is the set of feelings, beliefs and behaviour passed to you in your early years. Of course, during your childhood you will have received millions of messages. From birth until approximately the age of 10 your 'parent' ego state was very influential.

The parent ego state is often known as the 'taught' element. This influence may have come from your parents, relatives, teachers, older siblings, or other adults. In your early years you will have internalised many of the messages you received.

During your early years you were particularly receptive to the messages you repeatedly heard. These are the ones you internalised. Hopefully you received a combination of positive and negative messages. You probably also received some neutral messages. If you heard mostly negative messages this is likely to have started your self-confidence issues.

Have you ever noticed you say things just as your parents do or did? You probably don't do this consciously and may not necessarily want to. Another example is that you may treat others as you were treated as a child. Are you ready to explore your parent ego state?

Exercise: My 'Parent' Ego State

The parent ego state is dominant in your early years of development. The purpose of this exercise is to identify how this ego state has influenced your self-confidence.

1. Read each message and tick the ones that feel like negative messages to you

a. Don't do that

b. Do as you're told

c. You're a clever boy/girl

d. Do as I say not as I do

e. Don't' think you're better than anyone else

f. Who do you think you are?

g. Well done, I'm proud of you

h. You should know better

i. Don't let yourself down

j. Don't let us down

k. I love you

l. Don't ask stupid questions

m. Children should be seen not heard

n. Always be polite to your elders

o. You're so clumsy

p. Don't show yourself up

q. Big boys don't cry

r. Learn to stick up for yourself

s. Don't do that as you might hurt yourself

t. Don't raise your voice to me

u. Don't show us up

2. Now read all of these messages again. This time identify which of these messages you remember receiving regularly as a child

3. Do you use any of these expressions on your children or other people you interact with? If so, you're currently transferring these messages to others. Are you going to try to break your negative messaging?

4. What emotions are you feeling as a result of doing this exercise? Has it brought back any childhood memories? If so, are they good or bad memories?

5. Do you believe these negative messages are true, or have you just programmed your brain to accept them? Be honest with yourself

6. How have these negative messages influenced your self-esteem or self-confidence in your life so far?

7. Are you going to allow these messages to shape your future? It's time to decide what action you're going to take to tackle any of these negative messages you relate to. If you don't tackle these negative messages your progress to greater self-confidence will be stifled

A simple way to deal with these negative messages is to release them. Consciously let these messages go. Visualise them flying out of your mouth and drifting into the Universe. Tell yourself (in a kind voice) that these messages no longer serve any purpose for you.

You may need to repeat this exercise several times before those pesky negative thoughts disappear. Know that holding onto negative thoughts will make it difficult to improve your self-confidence.

If you think you can't do this, remind yourself that self-confidence is the best gift you can ever give yourself. By letting these thoughts go you're making space for new and better messages. The less emotional clutter you carry the more capacity you have for good experiences.

Note: the parent ego state has nothing to do with being a parent. Some business owners and managers use this ego state as their management style. This is not a recipe for successful leadership. Business leaders and managers who adopt this leadership style kill creativity and stop their staff taking the initiative. If this is you, it's time to revise your management style.

The 'adult' ego state is the result of your experiences and things that have influenced you so far. It's also about decision making, problem solving and your adaptability to the here and now. All your experiences, perceptions and reasoning merge to form the adult ego state.

This is often known as the 'thought' element. The adult ego state will be involved in much of the work you do in this book. Don't confuse the parent and adult ego states.

Do you find yourself saying "I must...", "I need to..." or "I should..."? These messages indicate resistance and reluctance as they are things you feel you should do rather than want to. Here are some typical examples of negative messages:

- I must go and see...
- I should be better at this
- I must clean the house
- I need to go grocery shopping
- I need to do the ironing
- I must finish... before I take a break
- I must contact...
- I need to get this report finished
- I must...
- I have to...

The list is not exhaustive. Do you have any of your own examples you want to add to this list?

These messages help reinforce your values as an adult. Negative messages can cause you to be too hard on yourself and so harm your self-confidence. In order to achieve sustainable self-confidence you need to strike a balance of positive, negative and neutral messages.

Clearly you can't change the past. However, if you allow childhood criticism to reinforce your adult thinking it will lower your self-esteem and self-confidence. Your self-confidence can't blossom if your parent or adult ego state keeps telling you that you're unworthy, unimportant or inferior.

In childhood some of your self-confidence came from the influential adults in your life. In adult life it's easy to blame your spouse, other family members, colleagues, friends or acquaintances for your lack of self-confidence. This is just an act of denial and won't give you a long-term solution.

You may well have some destructive people in your adult life, but this is your choice. If these people genuinely cared about you they wouldn't be trying to destroy your self-confidence. These scars aren't visible to the naked eye, but they are damaging none the less.

If you believe other people are trying to damage your self-confidence, consider the following:

- Your perception is wrong. These people aren't trying to drag you down; it's just your perception
- You like being a victim (yes I know this sounds harsh). At a deep level you thrive on this pain and so draw destructive people towards you
- The people dragging your down have their own self-confidence issues. Because they lack self-confidence they feel the need to drag other people down too

Having identified which is the true situation, what are you going to do about it? I'll leave that thought with you.

"Success is most often achieved by those who don't know that failure is inevitable" - Coco Chanel

The 'child' ego state is what makes you spontaneous, curious and affectionate. It's also your ability to be creative and how you receive messages. This ego state holds positive and negative memories too.

There are actually two child ego states. These are the natural or free child ego state and the adapted child ego state. There is plenty of information available if you wish to study ego states in detail.

Each time you receive a message your child ego state decides how you feel. This is often known as the 'felt' element. Your child ego state invokes the 'fight' or 'flight' response. This response can be triggered by both real and imaginary threats.

Having a basic understanding about the three primary ego states is useful. Having this knowledge means you act in awareness rather than blindly. This allows you to make changes in your behaviour.

Pause for a moment and think about how many times today you may have been in your child ego state. Here are some useful clues:

- Did you feel young again? Perhaps you did something that you remember from your childhood

- Were there any times today when you were doing what you were told to do? Did you rebel against anything today? Or, did you have a period of the day when you were just carefree?
- Did you behave like a child today? Perhaps you sulked about something or did something childlike
- Were you being your own self and just getting on with things in your own way?

How good are you at connecting with your child ego state? If you're not sure, try the following exercise:

Exercise: My 'Child' Ego State

This exercise requires using your imagination and thinking creatively. Imagine yourself as a toddler or young child. At this point in your life you haven't internalised self-confidence issues. For the next 10 minutes you're going to see what you experience as this very young person.

1. Set a timer for 10 minutes. The first part of this exercise is intended to be quick thinking

2. What are the feelings you're experiencing as this very young person? Typical examples include - happy, sad, scared, excited, curious, jealous, frustrated, affectionate, sulky or moody, confused, loving or compliant. Add as many feelings to this list as you can think of in 10 minutes

3. This is your blueprint. Each of these feelings still exists within you. Now look at your list and identify each feeling as positive (P) or negative (N). How often do you experience the positive feelings you've identified?

4. Whenever you experience a blip in your self-confidence revisit the positive feelings on your list. Allow these positive feelings to wash over you. This won't give you a long-term solution, but it will provide a temporary respite from your negative mindset. Sometimes this is all we need to kick start us

The messages that you remember are the ones you have internalised as part of your belief system. These recorded messages form a strong part of your personality. They also influence your behaviour as an adult. You will replay these messages to yourself, but you will also communicate them to others.

Now consider the impact of your internalised messages on you as an adult. For example, many people declare public speaking is their greatest fear. Of course there may be lots of reasons for this. Typically it's the messages you received and internalised as a child.

Did you internalise any of the following messages as a child?

- Don't show off
- No one likes a show-off
- You shouldn't boast
- Self-praise is no praise
- Who do you think you are?
- Don't draw attention to yourself

Have you noticed the common theme with these messages? Each one tells you it's wrong to be the centre of attention. The end result is - as an adult, being the centre of attention sends you into a panic.

Before moving on you might like to go back to the 'My Parent Ego State' exercise and ask yourself the following questions:

- Do I sometimes replay these 'parent ego' messages and allow them to influence the way I behave?
- Why do I allow these messages to prevent me from developing self-confidence?
- What satisfaction do I gain from hanging onto these negative messages?

At some deep level these negative messages are satisfying you. Be honest with yourself; do you enjoy being a martyr? Perhaps it's a way of getting attention as you hope people will notice you or feel sorry for you.

Ben has very kindly given me permission to share his story of ego with you, including his reluctance to do the exercises.

Case Study: The problem with ego

It's funny; when I first looked at the ego exercises my immediate thought was I don't have an ego. I immediately thought I don't need to do these exercises as I don't have any ego issues. Then I decided to do them anyway, out of curiosity.

Wow, I had spent my entire life believing that ego was an over-inflated sense of self-worth. Only now do I realise that ego has been a big part of my life. I now know that ego is the opposite of what I thought it was. I now know that ego is a bad thing. Ego destroys self-confidence like gangrene running through your body.

I don't believe my parents set out to be a poor example; I think they were just dysfunctional. I believe two people got together to have some fun but failed to take the necessary precautions. Then the inevitable happened and my mum got pregnant.

These two ill-equipped people decided to 'do the right thing' (as it was called then) and build a life together for the three of us. Both blamed me for what they saw as their future dreams being crushed. That didn't stop them having two more children though.

Up to the age of 18 my life was littered with lots of negative messaging. The messages I remember most clearly are:

- Children should be seen not heard
- No one likes a bragger
- Make sure you don't waste the opportunities you're given. We never had the chances you've got
- Don't bring your problems home
- You'll never do anything with your life; you're just like your mother/father (depending upon which one was saying it)
- You're too stupid to go to university or college - get a job
- We've looked after you all your life, now it's time for you to look after us
- Don't show off
- Who do you think you are? You're no better than the rest of us
- Self-praise is no recommendation
- How did your ego get so big?

Growing up in this environment, I had no idea how destructive these comments could be. I just thought this was normal behaviour, and all parents were like this. Being the eldest, I think more of these comments were directed at me than my siblings.

By the time I started my own family I realised that my parents hadn't been good role models for me or my siblings. I decided that I would never do this to my children, and I haven't. I've tried hard to create a loving and supportive home for my family. I think I've done a pretty good job really.

Recently I've discovered that I still have major self-esteem issues, which affect my self-confidence. I've also begun to realise that I have passed some of my issues onto my children. I never would have done this knowingly.

Although I tried not to make my parents mistakes, my own lack of self-confidence was obviously visible to my, now grown-up, children. I see my children share some of my confidence issues and then I feel guilty. Here I am in my fifties now trying to address a lifetime of ego bashing. I believe I will succeed but I wish I'd dealt with this years' ago.

(Ben - The problem with ego author)

If you wish to know more about ego states there are plenty of books available on Transactional Analysis, Neuro Linguistic Programming and Psychology.

"Believe in yourself! Have faith in your abilities! Without a humble but reasonable confidence in your own powers you cannot be successful or happy" - Norman Vincent Peale

5. Reasons For A Lack Of Self-confidence

"When you're a beautiful person on the inside, there is nothing in the world that can change that about you. Jealousy is the result of one's lack of self-confidence, self-worth, and self-acceptance" - Unknown

Let's be honest; lack of self-confidence is not a feel good experience. What's more lack of self-confidence is harmful to your sense of wellbeing. Why would anyone choose this when there's a better option available?

Before you can develop sustainable self-confidence you need to understand, and deal with, your lack of self-confidence. We all experience a lack of self-confidence at some point in our lives. It's important to understand this so you don't end up believing you're the only one.

It's hard to build self-confidence without first understanding the cause(s) of your lack of self-confidence. Lack of self-confidence can occur for lots of reasons. I have just listed some of the most common reasons. Consider if any of these apply to you:

- People saying unkind things to you or about you
- Physical disabilities or something else that makes you different
- Redundancy or being unable to get a job
- Parental or peer pressure
- Choosing to be a stay-at-home parent and losing your own identity. Note: not every stay-at-home parent experiences this
- Negative messaging in childhood from the influential adults in your life
- Fear of failure, fear of change or even fear of success. Some people just don't handle change well
- A traumatic life event
- Lack of self-belief
- Fear of criticism
- Self-doubt
- Feeling inferior or feeling unloved
- Unrealistic expectations or perfectionism
- Accepting defeat, or a lack of willingness to dig deep and persist to achieve your goals
- Justifying your flaws instead of working on them

- Victim of bullying or abuse (including workplace, social or domestic abuse)
- Lack of relevant skills or product knowledge
- Living in the shadow of a more confident friend, colleague or family member

You may have your own reasons for lack of self-confidence that I haven't included here. Before moving on, stop for a few minutes and consider your reasons for a lack of self-confidence.

Understanding the reasons for your lack of self-confidence is an essential step if you're going to find a permanent solution. Don't be judgemental. Accept whatever you observe.

Lack of self-confidence often starts in early childhood as children can be unbelievably cruel. In the classroom or school playground there always seems to be one child that doesn't quite fit in for whatever reason. You may have been that child, or you may remember a child from your school days.

For many people childhood is their first memory of self-confidence issues. We all need to internalise a belief that we have talents and abilities in order to develop self-confidence. For children this internalising happens from the encouragement they receive from the adults in their life.

Psychologists Bruce and Clyde Narramore have written various articles for Psychology for Living magazine. One article states "if a youngster doesn't receive adequate encouragement throughout childhood he/she may internalise this ongoing message and struggle with lack of confidence". Their article makes it clear how important it is for children to receive encouragement.

Early childhood experiences play a big part in creating feelings of inferiority. Did your parents provide a supportive environment or were they incapable of doing this? Were your parents demanding or over protective? Did you grow up in an environment of mostly positive or negative messages?

If your experience was lots of criticism and negative messages it's almost certain to have negatively impacted your self-confidence. Equally if your parents were demanding or overprotective this will probably have added to your negative perception of yourself.

What is your earliest lack of self-confidence memory? Is this memory one of the causes of your lack of self-confidence? This exercise might help you shed some light on your lack of self-confidence.

Exercise: My Earliest Memory

Self-confidence issues can start at any age. Often they start at a very young age. As life goes on we collect more baggage on the way. What's your earliest or strongest memory of a lack of self-confidence?

This exercise might take some time to complete. It may bring out some uncomfortable memories, long ago forgotten. Just remember, no experience is wasted. By revisiting these old memories you have the opportunity to release them and make a more positive future.

You will need a piece of paper and a pen for this exercise.

1. Identify your earliest or strongest lack of self-confidence memory

2. Imagine you're writing this as a story. Include as much detail as possible in your story so you're painting a clear picture. This is all part of the healing process. Note: it's fine to get upset

3. How did the situation make you feel at the time? How long did it take you to get over this experience? Did you get over it, or did it become a vivid memory that has stayed with you?

4. When you're ready, do a short meditation on your story. As you meditate, release your memories. Don't try to suppress them; just imagine them flying away. Keep meditating until you feel ready to stop. Your intuition will guide you

5. At the end of your meditation tell yourself that you're OK as you are. Know this issue no longer holds any power over you. You're now free to create new positive memories

You can't rewind history and change the past no matter how much you want to. Perhaps some of the people who created your unhappy memories feel guilty now. They can't change the past either.

The good news is the future doesn't have to be more of the same. You can choose a happier and more positive future, but this decision is yours. Releasing your old memories will free you up to develop self-confidence and a more positive future.

Mandy was one of my clients several years ago. As part of our work together Mandy identified that her issues started in her early childhood. She's kindly permitted me to include her case study.

Case Study: Reasons for my lack of self-confidence

When I was a client of Liz's she asked me where my lack of self-confidence came from. She asked me to think back to my earliest lack of self-confidence memory.

This led me to doing some serious soul searching, which brought things to light I wasn't aware of. A poignant exercise, but I'm glad I did it now.

I was brought up in a loving home in a remote part of the country. We had next door neighbours, but beyond that no neighbours for several miles.

Due to our remote location I had no regular playmates. I didn't go to nursery, playgroup or other pre-school activities. This wasn't because my parents didn't care; it's because they couldn't afford it. This led to me being painfully shy and struggling to comfortably interact with other children when I did encounter them.

My first regular contact with other children was when I went to school. What a culture shock that was for me. Firstly, I wasn't used to being away from my mum and hated it. Secondly, the other children in the class already knew each other. Thirdly, I didn't know how to socialise with other children.

My early experiences of school were feelings of isolation. I was the kid that stands out for being different. I was painfully shy, and often felt quite overwhelmed by this. At that time society wasn't so emotionally tuned into 'feelings'. I just had to cope with it to the best of my ability.

My memory is of me spending play time alone as I didn't know how to invite myself to join in. The other kids didn't invite me to play as they were just getting on with it. Many years later I realised that children don't wait to be invited, they just join in. I didn't have the confidence to do this though.

As I hadn't had much pre-school interaction I didn't naturally shine in the classroom either. I kept my head down, worked hard and said very little. Unfortunately for me, teachers and other adults didn't recognise my shyness. Instead they thought I was aloof and didn't want to join in. Oh how wrong they were!

Going to school and interacting with other children daily eventually worked its magic. Little by little I started to come out of my shell and developed a small circle of friends.

From this point on, this is how things remained at school. I remained quiet and had a small circle of friends. I rarely put my hand up in class, never took the initiative and remained largely unnoticeable. I was fine with this as I felt safe in this comfortable rut.

The other thing that peppered my childhood was the school bully. Every school seemed to have one. She (yes it was always a girl, never a boy) seemed to be drawn to me like a magnet. I went to four schools in total, and at each one I was singled out for 'special attention'.

It never occurred to me to tell anyone so nothing was done about it until secondary school. At this particular school, the bully came unstuck. On my behalf, someone reported her to the head teacher. Suddenly the bullying stopped.

On reflection, every school report talked about me needing to be more outgoing. At that time, no one thought about coaching or counselling to deal with my issues.

I'm not as shy now as I was back then, but I still do have some issues at large events. I still prefer to avoid large groups, and only have a small network of friends and acquaintances.

Don't get me wrong, I'm very happy with my life. I just wish I hadn't been so painfully shy as a child as it certainly started many of my self-confidence issues.

By revisiting my childhood memories I was able to objectively analyse them. I can't change the past. I may not do anything different in future; I haven't decided yet. What I have done is released some memories I wasn't aware I was hanging onto. This has freed up some space in my head for other memories. It's been quite liberating.

If I had one piece of advice for anyone with confidence issues it would be - 'tackle your issues as soon as possible. Just be brave and go for it. The relief you feel afterwards is worth it'.

(Mandy - Reasons for my lack of self-confidence author)

"Each of us has something we don't feel confident about. Don't let this hold you back" - Elizabeth J Tucker

As I've already said, your childhood is almost certain to have impacted your adult life in some way. You don't need to have had a bad childhood to have confidence issues from this time. Some parents are well intentioned but overprotective. While trying to be kind they can inadvertently smother your self-confidence.

Other parents seem to take the sledgehammer to crack a nut approach. I'm sure you've heard comments like "I don't praise him/her as it will only go to his/her head". If you constantly receive this message you grow up believing you're not capable or smart enough to overcome life's challenges.

Unfortunately, often self-confidence issues aren't dealt with at a young age, and so these issues are taken into adulthood. Sometimes children don't share their confidence issues with their parents and siblings. Sometimes parents don't know what to say or do about the situation. At times parents are the perpetrators of the emotional harm done.

If your parents lacked self-confidence then you're more likely to struggle with this too. If your parents didn't demonstrate their belief in your abilities as a child, you won't either. If you don't stop this destructive cycle you could pass on the same issues to your children.

The following exercise is an opportunity to reflect on your own childhood. This is not designed to be a 'blame my parents for everything exercise'. It's simply an opportunity to objectively reflect on your childhood memories - good or bad.

Whatever you discover from this exercise, it's an opportunity to move forward positively. It's your choice whether you want to tackle your self-confidence issues or not. You can't change the past but you can choose to positively influence your future.

Obviously as a life coach I would encourage everyone to create a positive future. However, I respect my clients' right to make their own decisions. The same rules apply to you. I hope your desire to change is strong enough to motivate you.

Exercise: I'm Just Like My Parents

Have you ever taken the time to think how much like your parents you are? Occasionally we say, think or do things like our parents. A thought might pop into your head - "I'm just like my mother/father". This exercise is going to take this thinking a step further.

You can do this exercise as a visualisation, or write your thoughts down. The choice is yours.

1. It's widely accepted that our parents and other adults influence our thinking as children. Some of their thought transference will be positive and some will be negative. Sit quietly and spend a few minutes reflecting on your childhood. Don't try to influence or judge your thoughts, just allow them to come and go

2. What are some of the things you say or do, which you have copied from your parents? This can be mannerisms or expressions copied from your parents or other influential adults. These may be positive or negative traits. Don't be judgemental - just acknowledge your observations

3. Review your thoughts or list. What positive habits have you adopted from the influential adults in your life? For example, you give people sincere compliments when an opportunity arises

4. Which negative habits have you learnt from the influential adults in your life? For example, do you say "no one likes a bragger"?

5. Which list is longer? Don't justify this. Remember this is just an observation exercise

6. Do you want to break free from the negative habits? If so, what are you going to do to break free from your negative habits/expressions?

7. Do the positive habits make you feel good or invoke happy memories? If so, spend a few moments acknowledging these positive role models. Remember the influence they've had on your life

8. Finally, consider the influence you're having on your children or other young people around you. Are you a positive role model for them?

"A mother who radiates self-love and self-acceptance actually vaccinates her daughter against low self-esteem" - Naomi Wolf

Lack of self-confidence can be a short or long-term experience, depending on when you choose to deal with the issues. For most it's unpleasant but it isn't debilitating. However, for others a lack of self-confidence is a major obstacle in their life.

Being trapped in a lack of self-confidence is not an uplifting experience and will almost certainly hold you back. Life is meant to be experienced. Don't stand on the side-lines watching your life passing by.

The perception of 'no choice' is one of the biggest inhibitors of self-confidence. If you believe you have no choice it can be mentally paralysing. This perception then stops you breaking free. Remember, it's only a perception.

The truth is you do have a choice. You can choose to be self-confident. Don't allow yourself to become a victim of circumstance. Otherwise lack of self-confidence will become a self-fulfilling prophecy that will severely restrict your life.

Breaking negative habits may be difficult initially. Stick with it as the end result will leave you with an increased sense of wellbeing. A sense of wellbeing is great for building self-confidence.

If your lack of self-confidence starts at a very young age then any future traumatic events are likely to affect you. For some their confidence issues start in their teens. Being dumped by your first love may create a temporary lack of self-confidence. The good news is teenagers tend to recover quickly as someone new generally appears soon afterwards.

As discussed at the start of the chapter there are common reasons for lack of self-confidence. There are also some common feelings we experience when we lack self-confidence. Do you experience any of the following when you're in a low self-confidence situation?

- Embarrassment or awkwardness - Yes/No
- Fear or panic - Yes/No
- Feel powerless - Yes/No
- Feel pessimistic or negative - Yes/No
- Feel tense or anxious - Yes/No
- Seem to be misunderstood - Yes/No
- Are let down by others - Yes/No
- Feel guilty - Yes/No
- Blame others - Yes/No
- Experience isolation or loneliness - Yes/No
- In awe of others if they appear confident - Yes/No

- Feel jealous or envious of confident people - Yes/No

It's good to be able to recognise when lack of self-confidence appears in your life. You may not experience all of these but when you do take action.

Hopefully you now have a clear idea of why you lack self-confidence and what you experience during these periods. Knowing the reason for your lack of self-confidence is an essential part of overcoming your confidence issues. Pat yourself on the back for being brave enough to go through this process.

Of course simply identifying the problem doesn't fix it. My question to you is what are you going to do about it? Understanding the reasons and the feelings you experience is only part of dealing with the problem of lack of self-confidence. Are you ready and willing to make changes for a more confident future?

You may not feel ready to do more than reflect on your lack of self-confidence right now. If so, be kind to yourself. You may have been on an emotional journey. Why not come back to this in a few days. You may feel ready to move forward then.

"Whether you come from a council estate or a country estate your success will be determined by your own confidence and fortitude" - Michelle Obama

Self-confidence doesn't just appear, as if by magic. It takes times, effort and commitment, but we all have to start somewhere. Considering what your future might look like seems like a pretty good starting point to me.

Exercise: My Future

Imagine what your future would look like if you made the decision to be confident. Allow your creative juices to start working and your mind to dream big. When you're ready answer the following questions. You will need paper and a pen for this exercise.

Answer each of the following questions as if you're now bursting with self-confidence. Don't allow your mind to drift back to your current lack of self-confidence. For this exercise everything is possible.

1. How would the new confident you walk around? How different is this to the way you walk around now? Think about your posture and body language

2. How would the new confident you talk? Think tone, volume, speed, choice of words. How different is this compared to the way you currently talk?

3. How would the new confident you feel inside? How does this compare with how you currently feel?

4. What would family, friends, colleagues, acquaintances and even strangers say about you? How is this different to what people currently say about you?

5. If you walked into a party or room full of strangers what would the new confident you do that you don't do now? How would this feel?

Thinking about your answers to these five questions, are you sufficiently inspired to take action? I'm not suggesting this will be an easy task, but if the rewards are high enough you're more likely to feel inspired.

You're now standing at a crossroads and only you can decide which way to go. Up until now you may have assumed that your lack of self-confidence wasn't optional. Perhaps you viewed it as a 'fait accompli'.

Now you know it is optional. So, what do you want to do? Do you want everything to stay the way it is? Or, do you want to make self-confidence your friend and future partner? You may decide you can't face making the changes right now. Applaud your honesty and know you can come back to this when you're ready to move forward.

Your negative perceptions and lack of self-confidence will stay with you throughout your life unless you tackle them. Give yourself permission to be the confident person you deserve to be. This change can be liberating, or even life changing. Just know you're worth the effort.

"Inaction breeds doubt and fear. Action breeds confidence and courage. If you want to conquer fear, do not sit at home and think about it. Go out and get busy" - Dale Carnegie

6. Lack Of Self-Confidence - Common Traits

"You have to believe in something so it might as well be you. It's great for your self-confidence" - Elizabeth J Tucker

Are you aware that people who lack self-confidence share common traits? Perhaps you haven't ever thought about this before. Consider if any of these common lack of self-confidence traits apply to you. People who lack self-confidence...

- Often avoid challenging tasks
- Believe tasks are beyond their ability, before they even try them
- Only set themselves goals they believe they can easily achieve
- Rarely reach their full potential
- Constantly compare themselves to others (generally less favourably)
- Focus too much attention on negative thoughts
- Lack the skills to be a positive role model for others
- Demonstrate defensive body language
- Give reasons for their actions (even if the outcome was a good one)
- Rush to immediately respond to criticism, instead of considering its merit first

The sooner you know what your lack of self-confidence traits are the sooner you can tackle them. If you recognise some of these traits in yourself don't just bury your head in the sand. Self-confidence is waiting for you when you're ready to embrace it.

The following exercise is an opportunity for you to identify the lack of self-confidence traits that apply to you. Don't be tempted to use this as an opportunity to beat yourself with a stick.

Exercise: My Lack of Self-confidence Traits

This questionnaire will help you to understand which common traits apply to you. Don't be overly critical as this is unhelpful. Just accept your responses to these questions. The goal is to inspire you to be confident, not add to your existing issues.

You will need a piece of paper and a pen for this short exercise.

1. Read each question in turn and answer Yes or No according to which best describes you

a. Whether I do something well or make a mistake I feel the need to explain my decision - Yes/No
b. I'm very hard on myself when I make a mistake - Yes/No
c. When something goes wrong I look to blame someone (myself or someone else) - Yes/No
d. I sometimes see myself as a victim of circumstance from my past experiences - Yes/No
e. I have a tendency to view all feedback as criticism - Yes/No
f. I become defensive whenever someone criticises me (even if the comments are from someone whose opinion I don't respect) - Yes/No
g. My view of life is glass half empty rather than glass half full - Yes/No
h. I regularly compare myself to other people - Yes/No
i. I take criticism personally and rarely see any value in the feedback I'm receiving - Yes/No
j. When I face difficulty I feel hopeless and negative - Yes/No
k. If something looks difficult I try to avoid doing it - Yes/No
l. When I overcome an obstacle I think about the lessons I've learned - Yes/No

2. Were the majority of your answers 'yes' or 'no'? The only question that should have a 'yes' answer is 'l'. If the majority of your responses were yes you are demonstrating many common lack of self-confidence traits

Before moving on, reflect on why you're so hard on yourself. What do you gain from this self-sabotage? How long have you been doing this?

A fear of criticism only occurs when you're too concerned about other people's opinions and feel insecure. The problem is most people become defensive when receiving criticism. It would actually be more helpful to view it as feedback. This allows you to analyse the value of the feedback and discard it if you feel it's incorrect.

When you care too much what others think you're open to manipulation. When you care less about what others think you become more honest as you don't need to pretend so much. This enables you to feel better about yourself, regardless of the facts. By breaking this habit you feel empowered.

"What would you do if you were immune to other people's opinions? Have the self-confidence to know only your opinion really counts" - Elizabeth J Tucker

Do your parents or peers have unrealistic expectations? If so, this pressure may lead to a lack of self-confidence if you're constantly striving to live up to their expectations. You may have developed a need to not disappoint them. This is hard to live with constantly.

Having unrealistic expectations of yourself is also damaging to your self-confidence. You may be putting yourself under unnecessary pressure. In short, regardless of who is responsible, unrealistic demands and expectations contribute to a lack of self-confidence.

Feelings of inferiority are a major cause of insecurity and a common lack of self-confidence trait. Childhood experiences can play a big part, but you can experience an inferiority complex at any age. Someone once said that they had an inferiority complex but it wasn't a very good one. This may be a joke but it has a serious point.

Feeling unloved or inferior often leads to a lack of self-esteem and lack of self-confidence. Have you got into the habit of feeling inferior to others? If so, this trait can make you feel inferior about anything. Scary isn't it.

Regardless of age, being ignored or ridiculed creates self-doubt and feelings of being unloved or inferior. Feeling inferior is also linked to a sense of shame, a feeling that you're at the bottom of the pack. Do you ever feel that you're not moving towards the top in anything?

As humans we're very aware of status, even if we pretend not to be. We often use expressions like 'one-upmanship', 'put down' or 'dis' (short for disrespect). How often do you use these expressions?

An inferiority complex makes you constantly worry about what others think of you. How often does this lack of self-confidence trait feature in your life? Do you devote as much time and attention to what you think of you?

Do you also spend time considering what you think of others too? In fact, do you spend too much time making judgements about yourself and others? Why not spend more time just being you. Overcoming your inferiority complex will be good for your self-esteem and self-confidence.

Perfectionism is another lack of self-confidence trait and a curse. It's like repeatedly hitting the self-destruct button. Constantly seeking perfection is hard work and leads to you having unrealistic expectations. More importantly, it will harm your self-confidence.

Thinking that you can't do something unless it's perfect is an unrealistic and unhelpful approach to life. It's also a way of avoiding making mistakes as you don't try new things. Always aspire to do your best, but don't become obsessive about it.

Perfectionists sometimes fool themselves into believing they live in a perfect world, and so try to do everything perfectly. This is like trying to knit fog - it's an impossible dream. If this is you it's time to tackle this negative habit. Constantly striving for perfection will damage your self-confidence.

"We all make mistakes - that's life. It's not a reason to go into a self-confidence nosedive" - Elizabeth J Tucker

Lack of assertiveness is another common lack of self-confidence trait. If you're not naturally assertive, does your behaviour tend to be passive or aggressive?

If you can't clearly express your needs and stand up for yourself you may become resentful and angry. A lack of assertiveness creates insecurity, doubt and pessimism. This then manifests itself as either passive or aggressive behaviour.

When you develop assertiveness skills people will realise you know your own mind. You will immediately have a more positive opinion of yourself. This will also lead to greater respect from others. Win/win!

The need to explain is a common lack of self-confidence trait. If this is your habit, take a moment to reflect. Do you always feel the need to explain, or just in certain situations? Has this become an automatic response to what has been said to you? Why do you feel the need to explain? How do you feel afterwards? Try to become aware of it happening in future. This will give you the opportunity to stop it.

The need to explain is a habit that can spiral out of control if it's not checked. You start off by explaining when you make a bad decision. Then you start explaining your good decisions. Before you know it you will be giving an explanation for everything you do. All the while you're eroding your self-confidence.

Making excuses is another common indicator of lack of self-confidence. Are you wondering if this describes you? If so, answer this question: If you drop something, or knock something over, do you immediately give a reason for it? Everyone has accidents and mishaps. Confident people don't feel the need to say anything.

Do you find yourself justifying every error of judgement or mistake you make? Don't immediately rush to justify yourself when something goes wrong. You're human and no-one expects you to be perfect all the time. Give yourself a break.

Are you too self-critical when you have an accident? Do you immediately say something like 'I'm so clumsy' or 'I'm so stupid'? This self-sabotage is unhelpful and simply serves to undermine your self-confidence. If this is one of your traits, stop it now.

Blaming others or constantly complaining about others is another common sign of lack of self-confidence. The complainer tries to shift the responsibility and put the blame on those they are complaining about. This creates a negative atmosphere that affects everyone involved. The complainer with low self-esteem or low self-confidence often becomes a victim.

Any kind of negative thinking and negative messaging is another common lack of self-confidence trait. Constantly making negative comments about yourself, those around you and life in general doesn't make you good company. Of course your negativity may not be a self-confidence issue, but often it is.

Self-criticism is not an endearing habit. It will put people off wanting to be around you. This behaviour sends out two distinct messages. It says you either lack self-confidence or you're seeking attention using reverse psychology.

Do you constantly compare yourself to others? If so, do you always rate yourself less favourably? Always wanting to be like other people is exhausting and will never deliver sustainable self-confidence. You're unique – just enjoy being you.

Your friends like you, not who you aspire to be. Accept this with good grace, and stop this self-sabotage. Self-sabotage will destroy whatever self-confidence you have. By choosing to behave in this way you're simply make unnecessary work for yourself when you decide to improve your self-confidence.

When someone gives you feedback do you immediately assume it's criticism? Do you then become defensive and/or argumentative? If so, stop. This says 'lack of confidence' to the person giving you feedback.

Confident people accept that not all feedback is intended as criticism. They listen to the feedback as there might be some merit in it. If the feedback is valuable they accept it; otherwise they let the comments go. There's no sense in harbouring negative comments that serve no purpose. Learn to evaluate feedback and then respond not react to it.

These are just some of the most common traits of a lack of self-confidence. Many people won't recognise them as your lack of self-confidence. However, there will be lots of people who are aware of the signs.

Some will use this as a trigger to reach out and help you. Others will abuse this knowledge, and use it as a means to manipulate you. This is another good reason to tackle your lack of self-confidence.

Until you acknowledge your negative thoughts or behaviour you can't hope to overcome it. Here is an exercise to help you identify how frequently you're a negative thinker.

Exercise: Overcoming Negative Thoughts

It can be difficult to admit you're a negative thinker as this often affects how others see you. A good starting point is keeping a diary of your negative thoughts. For example, recording when you tell yourself you can't do something (often without even trying). This will identify how often you fall into the trap of negative thinking.

You may not like doing this exercise but the sooner you face up to your negative thinking the sooner you can break this emotionally harmful habit.

For this exercise you will need to keep a diary or journal. It's up to you how long you want to continue this exercise, but I recommend you do it for at least four weeks.

1. Each time you have a negative thought make a note of it in your diary or journal

2. Next, consider what has created your negative thinking? All negative thinking happens for a reason. For example you've been told you're unattractive or useless since childhood or you repeatedly make the same mistake etc

3. Now think about how you can overcome this negative belief. This may include asking someone else to help you, or rewarding yourself each time you turn a negative thought into a positive one. The solution is different for each of us

4. At the end of four weeks review your diary/journal. If successful you should notice your diary/journal has fewer entries towards the end of the exercise

5. You may like to continue with your diary/journal. Alternatively, you may now be in the habit of pulling yourself up when you drift into negative thinking

Note: this habit can be broken or at least lessened, but it takes time and effort. Don't give up after the first few days if you feel like you're not succeeding.

Personally I used a reward system to break the cycle of negative thinking. Each time I said or thought something negative I put £1 in a money box. This act of having to pay a forfeit made me much more aware of my negative thinking. When I finally broke the habit I emptied the money box and bought myself a present to celebrate. Shoes in my case!

Lack of self-confidence is common in men, women and children. However, it seems in the battle of the sexes women fall short in terms of self-confidence.

Women are generally more afraid of failure than men, according to a Global Entrepreneurship Monitor report. It's important to address this as self-confidence plays an important role in both personal and professional success. If lack of self-confidence is the only thing holding you back then surely this is a battle worth winning.

Research suggests that women often assume others are smarter than them, without any evidence to support this. The same research also suggests that women fear their employer finding out they don't deserve their position.

Does the previous paragraph describe you (whether you're male or female)? If so, spend a moment reflecting on how harmful this kind of thinking is to your self-confidence. Now spend a few moments reflecting on the opportunities that have slipped through your fingers as a result of lack of self-confidence.

You can't change the past, but you don't need to make the same mistakes in the future. Self-confidence wants to be your friend if you'll let it. Make yourself a promise not to allow this kind of negative thinking to scupper your chances in future.

"Don't give in to fear. Fear is paralysing and stops you being your authentic self. Speak up, be strong and be confident" - Elizabeth J Tucker

On the assumption that you have some self-confidence, are you internally or externally confident? If you're internally confident you aren't reliant on other people's positive feedback to motivate you. If you lack self-confidence or you're externally confident the chances are other people's opinions matter to you. This is fine as long as other people's opinions aren't more important than your own.

If you don't already know whether you're internally or externally confident, try this exercise and find out:

Exercise: Internal Versus External Self-confidence

It's important to start to build your internal confidence. To do this, every day consciously note those moments when you do something well or feel at your most confident. You may like to spend a few minutes at the end of the day reflecting on what went well today.

Acknowledging how good you are at something is a great confidence builder. This acknowledgement has nothing to do with ego. It's about being objective and learning to value what you have to offer.

You will need a piece of paper and a pen for this short exercise.

1. Read each question, but don't spend too much time thinking about the questions

2. Write the answer that automatically pops into your head

3. When you're ready, the questions are:

a. How do you know when you've done something well?

b. Do you rely on other people to tell you when you've done something well, or do you recognise it for yourself?

c. Do you acknowledge each of your successes? Or, do you just ignore them and move on to the next task? Acknowledgement is like a virtual pat on the back. We all need praise and encouragement

d. How important is praise from other people to you? Do you require praise from others to motivate you?

e. If other people don't praise you do you tend to assume you haven't done something well; or at least not well enough for recognition?

4. Now you've answered all five questions look at your answers. Decide how much do other people's opinions matter to you. Does your opinion matter or more less than other peoples? Now read the analysis:

Analysis:

Other people's opinions: If other people's opinions matter more than your own then your self-confidence is external. Too much dependence on others is bad for your self-confidence. It means that you will always need reassurance from other people. It's time to build some self-reliance. Of course praise from other people is nice and makes you feel good; just don't become reliant on it

Your opinion: If you're able to recognise when you've done something well pat yourself on the back. Internal self-confidence is much healthier than external self-confidence. When other people give you compliments accept them graciously. Never be tempted to bat compliments away as this may have a negative effect on the other person

In 'A Matter of Self-confidence - Part II' I've focused on the benefits of self-confidence and how to achieve it.

For now, develop your own self-confidence ritual. It doesn't need to be anything long or complicated. If you get the chance, spend a few minutes watching professional tennis players. You will notice they often bounce a ball three or four times before serving. This is a simple self-confidence ritual. Yours could be something as simple as a positive affirmation.

In the Appendices section (Chapter 10) I have included some affirmations to get you started.

"Don't let lack of self-confidence stop you putting your reputation on the line. How else will you grow?" - Elizabeth J Tucker

7. Self-confidence And Your Personal Beliefs

"Finding a belief in yourself will give you a feeling of being comfortable with who you are. Now that's what I call self-confidence" - Elizabeth J Tucker

Whether you recognise it or not your life is peppered with your personal beliefs. Most likely these will be a combination of positive and negative beliefs. Your personal beliefs are unbelievably powerful. Try not to regard your personal beliefs as good or bad. It's far more empowering to describe your beliefs as helpful or unhelpful.

We all have personal beliefs; they're a part of who we are. All too often people are unaware of the influence beliefs have on them. Does this describe you? Have you ever taken the opportunity to analyse, or even challenge, your personal beliefs?

Your self-limiting beliefs are the problem ones. These beliefs are one of the greatest barriers to self-confidence. If you search too deeply you can develop some self-limiting beliefs you didn't start out with. Therefore, tread with care.

Whether you like it or not your self-limiting beliefs can crush your self-confidence. If you keep adding to your list of self-limiting beliefs they may leave you feeling defeated. In extreme cases this can lead to emotional or mental health issues.

Self-confidence is not genetic; it's a matter of personal choice. You don't have to be reliant on others to increase your self-confidence. Whatever your self-limiting beliefs are they can be changed! I've included Isobel's story of overcoming her self-limiting beliefs.

Case Study: Overcoming my self-limiting beliefs

I have lacked self-confidence for as long as I can remember. I don't remember any particular event triggering this; it just seems to have been the elephant in the room for most of my life.

I decided that I would like to do some voluntary work, but I didn't feel I had the skills to do anything very adventurous or 'out there'. However, I am an efficient administrator so that's what I decided to do. I became a volunteer administrator at my local hospice.

When I became a hospice volunteer I assumed that I would be tucked away in an office somewhere. It never occurred to me that I would be on the reception desk welcoming visitors as part of my role.

At first I thought I wouldn't be able to do the receptionist's role due to my lack of self-confidence. The staff seemed completely oblivious to my confidence issues and treated me just like everyone else. I didn't know it at the time but they did me a favour.

I now volunteer twice a week at my local hospice. I'm a volunteer receptionist and administrator. I do all my duties in reception where I'm accessible to everyone. I had to overcome my self-confidence issues as I understand how difficult it is for visitors the first time they walk through the door

Our visitors are visiting people who are terminally ill. Many will never leave here alive. I need to give a confident and uplifting impression for their benefit.

As the receptionist, it's crucial that I help put visitors at ease. I recognise that I'm the 'shop window' of the hospice. If I create a bad first impression it will impact how visitors feel about the hospice as a whole. Being the receptionist has definitely helped me overcome some of my anxieties around others.

I make a concerted effort to welcome every visitor, and help them to feel relaxed. They don't want to take their fears and anxieties with them when they visit their family or friends. I'm not a naturally extrovert person, but somehow this role has drawn me out of myself.

I now find it much easier to interact with family, friends, and colleagues. I'm much friendlier and more confident joining in group discussions with my colleagues here and in my workplace. My work colleagues have started to notice and comment on how much more confident I appear lately. This makes me feel good and motivates me to try harder.

Somebody once told me about the ABC model. At the time it didn't mean much to me, but now it does. I've now begun to realise that my Attitude and Behaviour create the Consequences (positive or negative).

Historically I've been overlooked for promotions at work, even though I knew I was capable of doing the job. My attitude was 'I probably won't be considered for the job as there are better qualified applicants'. Sometimes I didn't even bother applying.

When I did apply I would go around telling everyone that I wouldn't get the job anyway. Inevitably this became a self-fulfilling prophecy. The interviewing manager got the impression that I wasn't really interested so didn't consider my application as seriously as they might have.

Since my self-confidence has grown I've changed my attitude and behaviour. I've started tackling some of my other self-limiting beliefs now too. The end result is I've also achieved my longed-for promotion. I love my new job and the new level of responsibility. I continue to volunteer at the hospice as I'm so grateful for the difference this role has made to my life.

If you're reading my story I assume you have issues with self-limiting beliefs too. I encourage you to step up to the plate and tackle your self-limiting beliefs. If you're like me you'll be glad you did.

(Isobel - Overcoming my self-limiting beliefs author)

The good news is personal beliefs aren't always true and aren't usually permanent. Self-limiting beliefs are like the bars to a prison. However, this self-confidence prison only exists in your mind. Unlike a physical prison you can break free without further punishment.

If your thinking is a constant reminder of failures, inadequacies or comparing yourself unfavourably to others your self-confidence is bound to suffer. Instead, focus on your achievements, personal growth, developments and successes. You will notice your confidence level is now much higher with this approach.

Here are some typical examples of how your self-limiting beliefs may sabotage your self-confidence:

All or nothing thinking - believing something is a total failure or a total success. Very few things in life are like this, so look for the middle ground. This kind of drama queen thinking is very unhelpful.

Over generalising - making sweeping statements based on one bad experience. Try to get things into perspective and see it for what it is - a single bad experience. Then move on. Don't hold onto the memory. Negative memories create unnecessary emotional clutter.

Exaggerating - don't turn a minor irritant or embarrassment into a major disaster. Accept in the grand scheme of things it's not that important. To quote Richard Carlson "don't sweat the small stuff".

Discounting the positive in favour of negative thoughts - recognise your skills and strengths. Learn to appreciate them (just as you would for family and friends). Also recognise the high esteem others have for you and your capabilities. This is not an ego trip; it's about learning to recognise your self-worth.

Catastrophizing - don't always imagine or expect the worst to happen. Most times this won't happen and these feelings are emotionally draining. On the rare occasions the worst does happen you will find a way to deal with it.

Did you recognise any of the above traits in yourself? If so, don't rush to beat yourself up or make excuses. Just accept them and vow to work on them.

The first step to overcoming self-limiting beliefs is understanding why you feel this way. Only when you understand 'why' can you find a way to fix the problem.

Spend a little time reflecting on why you harbour these self-limiting beliefs. They didn't just happen for no reason; so what was the trigger? You may not find the answer to this initially. In fact, you may revisit this many times before you find the answer.

The next step is to become aware of your self-talk. When you catch yourself having negative thoughts or making negative comments, stamp on them. Challenge yourself to replace every negative thought/comment with a positive one. Turn it into a game so it doesn't become a self-victimisation exercise.

It's hard to be confident if you don't think you'll do well at something. Imagine you're taking an exam. The more you believe in yourself the greater your chances of success. Think of your entire life as an exam, and make sure you're prepared to succeed every step of the way.

Confident people find ways to work around their self-limiting beliefs; particularly those regarding ability. You may find it easier to use alternative beliefs that will help and encourage you to achieve your goals. There is no right or wrong way to deal with personal beliefs. It's all about understanding you and deciding what works best for you.

Did your school reports always state things like 'could do better'? If so, the chances are you've grown up believing you're not as good as you could be. For some people this is a great motivator, but for most it has a negative impact.

Try to put 'could do better' into perspective. No one is perfect so it stands to reason things could be better. Accept the comment and move on. Life's too short to dwell on it.

Here's a short exercise to test your personal belief system. For this exercise imagine yourself going for a job interview.

Before you even arrive for your job interview your beliefs have come into your mind. You've already decided whether you're good at interviews of not. This thinking is likely to influence the outcome as it will affect your performance. At the same time you will be sending out silent messages to the interviewer.

Exercise: I'm Not Good at Interviews Versus I Present Myself Well at Interviews

All you need for this exercise is a piece of paper and a pen, plus a good imagination or memory.

1. Spend a few minutes thinking of an occasion, or occasions, when you've gone for a job interview, which didn't go well. You went into this interview telling yourself "I'm not good at creating a positive impression at interviews". Try to remember how this interview played out on the day, or imagine how it played out

2. Remember what your body language was like. The chances are you appeared very tense and uncomfortable. You may even have given off signals that suggested you were unfriendly. Did you smile? Were your answers short and abrupt etc?

3. How good were the examples you gave in the interview? Did you kick yourself afterwards - thinking of all the better examples you could have given?

4. Were you very quick thinking on the day, or did you struggle to come up with responses that answered the questions being asked? Were you so nervous you couldn't digest the questions properly?

5. How did your voice sound? Were you vibrant, confident and enthusiastic or were you uncertain? Did the nerves make your voice sound high-pitched? Or, were you almost whispering?

6. Although you may find it uncomfortable, or even painful, to reflect on this you can only move forward by acknowledging your issues

7. Write down all the thoughts or memories you have about this scenario

8. Now spend a few minutes reflecting on a job interview that went well. Think of a time when you got the job. If you've never experienced a positive job interview simply imagine how you might feel

9. What was your body language was like? Did you appear relaxed (or as relaxed as you can be in an interview) and comfortable?

10. How good were the examples you gave in the interview? Did you give some good examples that demonstrated your skills?

11. Were you quick thinking on the day, and able to answer the questions with relative ease?

12. Were you upbeat and enthusiastic? How convincing did you sound to yourself and the interviewer?

13. You obviously went into the interview with a more positive outlook as you were offered the job. Did you prepare better for this interview? Or, did you just believe the job was yours?

14. Write down all the thoughts or memories you have about this scenario

15. Spend a few minutes reflecting on these two scenarios and how you behaved

16. Now spend a few minutes reflecting on what you've learnt from this exercise. No one likes interviews but if you're going to be successful you've got to present yourself well

17. What will you do differently in future?

Although this exercise was based on a job interview the same principle applies to everything. The more positive and optimistic you are the better the outcome is likely to be.

Do you care too much about what others think of you? It might surprise you to know, but most people don't give you a huge amount of thought. That's not because they don't like you. Most people are just busy getting on with their own life and so don't dedicate a great deal of thinking time to others.

Generally people give little or no thought to how confident, or not, the people around them are. Add this to your own self-limiting beliefs and you're probably wasting too much time on negative thinking. Focus your attention on what you think, but make sure it's positive. Yours is the only opinion that really matters.

Giving up worrying about what other people think is liberating. Giving up your self-limiting beliefs is even more liberating. Go on; give yourself permission to stop being held back by your personal beliefs.

Think back to your childhood. On the whole children don't tend to worry about what others think of them until adults start brainwashing them. Children don't worry about making a fool of themselves either. If they did they would never learn to do anything.

When you start internalising the messages from others you suddenly start worrying more about what other people think than what you think. It's as if someone suddenly flicks a switch in your brain. This is such a shame as you often end up robbing yourself of the opportunity to fully embrace life.

Harvard University research suggests that around 90% of what we experience is not in the outside world. Their research suggests it's the result of how we see the world. Scary huh!

If you spend most of your time thinking about your shortcomings and what can go wrong you will lower your self-confidence. On the other hand if you focus on your strengths and think positive thoughts your confidence will be higher. Self-awareness is a good starting point for self-confidence. Make a conscious effort to become aware of the judgements you're making.

You may find it difficult to move from negative to positive thinking initially. If so, take this two-step approach to conquer your self-limiting beliefs. This is a penalty and reward system.

Step 1: Make a mental note each time you're having negative thoughts. When you have a negative thought put £1 in a 'negative thoughts' money box. This is a way of making you consciously aware of the habit so you can break it. The more it costs you the sooner you will want to break the habit

Step 2: When you've got into the habit of noticing your negative thoughts you can tackle them. Each time you have a negative thought challenge yourself to replace it with a positive one. Reward each success. This could be a single sweet, five minutes doing something you enjoy, or anything else you fancy

Once positive thinking becomes your new default position it's time to reward your success. Take the money from your 'negative thoughts' money box and buy yourself a present. Your new found self-confidence will probably still be fragile at this point. Rewarding your efforts will help reinforce your self-confidence. It's a bit like giving yourself a pat on the back.

Another exercise you might like to try is keeping a journal. Make a note every time you think people are judging you. Sometimes you will be right, but often you will be wrong. The chances are you will never know as you can't get inside someone else's head. In reality, these are your judgements not someone else's.

The important thing is you will become aware of when you think you're being judged. This will help you to break the habit of allowing other people's opinions to matter more than your own. Breaking this bad habit will lead to greater self-confidence.

In order to develop sustainable self-confidence you will need to develop some empowering personal beliefs. The not very confident you may struggle with this. Stick with it as the end result will be a new more confident you.

"If you crave winning and fear losing you're unlikely to achieve lasting self-confidence. In order to succeed you need to dream big and remove your self-limiting beliefs" - Elizabeth J Tucker

The first thing you need to do is neutralise your self-limiting beliefs. Here's an exercise to help you identify what your self-limiting beliefs are so you can eliminate them:

Exercise: My Self-limiting Beliefs

We may not like admitting it but we all have self-limiting beliefs. When your self-limiting beliefs stifle your self-confidence it's time to do something about it.

1. Set aside 20 - 30 minutes each day for a week. This is your quiet reflective time. Each day ask yourself the same question - "what are my self-limiting beliefs?"

2. Only ask this question, nothing else. If your mind wanders simply repeat the question to return your focus to it

3. During your reflective time write down any self-limiting beliefs that you have. Your list will probably have mostly the same issues each day, but you may have some different ones

4. At the end of the week review your list of self-limiting beliefs. Notice how often the same belief has appeared on your list; how often you're reinforcing this message

5. Choose just one self-limiting belief from your list (you can come back to the others another time). For example, "I can't do..." This can be the one you most want to overcome, or the easiest one to tackle. The choice is yours

6. Why do you have this self-limiting belief? Write down every thought you have that reinforces this belief. Were you told this as a child, do you keep making the same mistake etc?

7. Is there any real evidence to support this belief? If so, what is the evidence? If not, why have you become so attached to this self-limiting belief? For example, how do you know you can't do something? How often have you tried it? If you have tried and failed – how often?

8. What would it take to make you change your mind about this self-limiting belief? Don't say "guaranteed success". Success can't be guaranteed. The best you can hope for is increasing your chances of success

9. It's important to neutralise this self-limiting belief. Visualise yourself overcoming the belief and no longer being affected by it. For example - imagine your self-limiting belief is you will never pass your driving test. Now visualise yourself passing and ripping up the 'L' plates. Feel the excitement of passing your driving test. Now visualise the car you will buy yourself and see yourself driving it

10. Once you have successfully dealt with this self-limiting belief you can do the same exercise for every one you have. Imagine how great your life would be if you could neutralise all those destructive thoughts

Note: If you can successfully overcome one self-limiting belief you can overcome others too. I challenge you to try! If you would like to share your success stories, email me – shepherdcreativelearning@gmail.com

"Know that even the most confident people feel nervous or lack self-confidence sometimes. You're not alone" - Elizabeth J Tucker

Like everyone else, you have qualities, but if you lack self-confidence you probably tend to dismiss your qualities. At worst, you may also be oblivious of some of life's positive experiences. Here's a short exercise to address this:

Exercise: My Qualities and Positive Experiences

Positive thinking is a powerful tool for building self-confidence. Positive thinking on its own won't achieve self-confidence, but as one of your strategies it has a part to play. The point of this exercise is to make you more observant as well as help you to increase your self-confidence.

This exercise is not about ego; it's simply about honestly appraising your qualities. It's also an opportunity to reflect on when you did something that turned into a positive experience.

Think of a random act of kindness you did for someone. Did you encourage someone to do something, give up your seat on the train/bus, or buy The Big Issue etc? It doesn't matter what the act was. The point is this was an act of kindness that helped someone else. How did their gratitude make you feel at the time?

1. Write a short summary of a time when you demonstrated or experienced each of the following qualities:

- Courage
- Kindness
- Selflessness
- Love
- Sacrifice
- Wisdom
- Happiness
- Determination

2. If you can't think of an example for each one straightaway, come back to it another time

3. Review what you've written. As you do so, allow yourself a few minutes to savour the memory

4. How do you feel now you've completed this exercise? Was it difficult to do initially? Resistance is perfectly normal as you may feel as though you're blowing your own trumpet. Of course, you're not

5. You might like to store this somewhere safe. When your self-confidence is feeling a bit low, take this list out and read it for an instant confidence boost

The important thing to learn is only you can overcome your self-limiting beliefs as self-confidence comes from within you. The fewer self-limiting beliefs you harbour the greater your self-confidence will be.

"Develop an aura of self-belief that bullets would bounce off. It's great for your self-confidence" - Elizabeth J Tucker

8. Change, Fear And Self-confidence

"Change happens because someone makes it happen. Have the self-confidence to be in control of the change in your life" - Elizabeth J Tucker

In order to achieve your desired level of self-confidence you need to go through the change cycle. Often this change requires facing and overcoming your fears. As humans we learn through our experiences, not theory. All the theoretical knowledge in the world is useless if it's not put to use.

Change is coming. Greek Philosopher Heraclitus once said "The only thing that is constant is change". This is as relevant now as it was in the sixth century when he said it.

Change can be scary. It's full of unknowns and uncertainty. But, get to the other side of change and you'll discover new self-confidence. The rewards will make the effort worthwhile.

Here are some things you should know about change:

- Change is an emotional experience. You may experience one, some, or all of the following emotions during a period of change: On the plus side - excitement, happiness, motivation, or optimism. On the negative side - worry, depression, sadness, anger, fear or stress

- Change always means loss of some kind; even if it's just losing the negative stuff that holds you back

- In order for change to be a positive experience you have to reach the point of acceptance. Often this comes from having a clearer picture of the process or what the future might look like. Acceptance is frequently the hardest element of change to deal with

- Acknowledge that resistance to change is natural and normal. After all, generally change is going to take you outside your comfort zone for a period of time

- Change may be painful at the time. However, when you reflect on it afterwards you will have learnt something from the experience. There is a lesson in every change. Try to look back and find some positives when you've experienced change. A negative mindset will simply make your personal development much harder

---

There are lots of different examples of cycles of change. I've chosen this six step cycle to explain change as it's simple and easy to understand. I hope this will be of some use to you.

Step 1 - recognising the need for change, or that change is coming

Step 2 - clarification or a clear understanding of the situation. It's up to you whether you view this as an opportunity or a problem to be overcome

Step 3 - creating a plan of action. This actually gives you some control over the change

Step 4 - implementing your plan of action. Having a plan and doing something with it are very different things. Procrastination not only means nothing gets done, it also has the potential to erode your self-confidence or self-esteem

Step 5 - review your action plan regularly. This is a way of monitoring your physical progress and your emotional attitude to the changes you're undergoing

Step 6 - celebrate your success. As I've said before, reward is very important when building self-confidence

Your ability (or inability) to deal with change can say a lot about your outlook on life. So, how well do you normally cope with change?

Exercise: How Well Do I Cope With Change?

Change is inevitable; it's a natural part of our lives. As songwriter Johnny Rivers said "the only thing that's permanent is change". Sometimes the changes are very subtle and you don't notice them, but change is still happening.

All change carries uncertainty and an element of risk. Do you go with the flow or are you someone who has to be dragged kicking and screaming? If you know how you respond to change you can develop better coping strategies.

You may never find change exciting. However, if you can be a little less reluctant and not always drag your heels, you will find change less painful or challenging.

1. Read each question and answer Yes or No

a. When confronted by big changes I consider how people I admire handle change. I use them as my role models - Yes/No

b. I try to view change positively. I see it as something new and exciting - Yes/No

c. I take personal responsibility for my reaction to any changes that affect me - Yes/No

d. I realise that a positive change in one area of my life may not make my entire life better - Yes/No

e. I try to ensure that some aspects of my life remain the same if I have major changes to deal with - Yes/No

f. I believe change helps me to grow and develop - Yes/No

g. I can make changes in my life without other people's approval - Yes/No

h. I recognise that all change has an element of uncertainty, but I don't let fear of failure (or success) hold me back - Yes/No

i. I realise that sometimes even good changes may have unexpected problems - Yes/No

j. I recognise that some changes are beyond my control, but it's my choice to become a victim or not - Yes/No

k. During periods of change I seek help from my support network - Yes/No

l. If change is happening for family, friends or colleagues I offer whatever support I can - Yes/No

m. When I'm going through periods of change I consciously work on maintaining a sense of perspective - Yes/No

n. When I've been through a big change I take time out to reflect on the experience and identify what it's taught me - Yes/No

o. I'm comfortable letting go of the past but hold onto the memories I want to keep - Yes/No

p. When implementing change in my life I break it down into manageable chunks - Yes/No

q. I believe change is generally a mix of good and bad - Yes/No

2. Look at your answers. For each 'Yes' you scored give yourself 1 point

3. Add up your score and read the analysis below

Analysis:

---

0 - 5: You clearly don't cope with change very well. This probably increases your stress level, which is unhelpful for your physical and mental wellbeing. Your score suggests you need to develop some coping strategies. A good starting point is developing your support network and asking for help when you need it

6 - 11: You obviously cope with change fairly well, but you could develop better coping strategies. Consider whether there are specific areas of your life where you cope better. If so, focus on developing better strategies in the areas where you don't cope so well

12 - 17: You appear to embrace change positively and cope with it very well. Can you share your coping strategies with others to help them cope with change better?

4. Has your attitude to change always been the same? Or, has something happened to make you develop this positive or negative attitude?

5. If you scored less than 12 spend a few minutes considering what you can do to feel more comfortable with change in future. A positive attitude towards change will help with building your self-confidence

As humans we all have the capacity to cope with change (in varying degrees). You may need to remind yourself that you can't control every situation in your life, but you can cope with change.

Most situations are a combination of things you can change and things you can't change. The simple solution is to change what you can and learn to accept or deal with what you can't change. I know this sounds simplistic. I also recognise that this may be hard to do initially.

The good news is you have the ability to cope with change and be more confident as a result of it. Are you still feeling some resistance towards embracing change? If so, here are my top ten benefits of change. I hope they will go some way to persuading you that change is good:

- You grow and learn every time something changes in your life
- Change helps you to adapt to new situations, environments and people. As a result you're able to cope better when something unexpected happens
- Without change you can't expect improvements in your life. This could be work, relationships, finances or anything else
- Change sometimes helps you to re-evaluate your life, values or priorities

- Not all change has to be massive. If a change feels too big to tackle, break it down into smaller chunks. In the end the big change will happen anyway
- Not all changes lead to pleasant periods in your life, but this phase passes too. Life isn't a fairy tale but it is your personal story
- Change triggers progress. Things move forward and develop as a result of change
- Change sometimes provides new opportunities that wouldn't otherwise have been available to you
- Change is a bit like turning a page in the book of your life. Sometimes the change leads to a whole new chapter
- Without change we would never see beautiful butterflies or new life being born

Would you really choose a dull and predictable life over change? If so, you would then run the risk of dying of boredom!

There are three very common fears. These are fear of change, fear of failure and fear of success. We've already explored change so I won't dig any deeper into that topic.

Once you've tackled your resistance to change you may need to overcome your other fears. Sometimes you may need to step outside your comfort zone and take that leap of faith. It's fine to be scared; confidence is waiting on the other side of your fears.

Fear falls into two categories. These are rational fears and irrational fears. Both will feel equally real at the time. Both types of fear also create the same physical symptoms.

You need to decide whether your fear of change, failure or success is rational or irrational. I suspect your fears will probably be mostly irrational. It's perfectly normal to feel fearful or anxious on occasions so don't beat yourself up.

There are two aspects to fear and anxiety. These are your physical reactions and your emotional reactions. Physical reactions may include raised heartbeat, nausea, sweating or going red.

The emotional reactions are the thoughts that play out in your head. Do you have thoughts like 'I never know what to say to strangers' or 'my mind always goes blank in interviews' etc?

Don't let fear hold you back. It's too easy to use fear as an excuse to never challenge yourself. If you do you will never overcome your lack of self-confidence.

Ask yourself "would I really choose to live the rest of my life suffering from a lack of self-confidence"? Lack of self-confidence may stop you achieving your goals and dreams. It will almost certainly stop you enjoying the full range of life's opportunities available to you.

"Don't allow yourself to feel like a failure or feel frustrated with your efforts as this just erodes your self-confidence" - Elizabeth J Tucker

When I was doing the research for this book I asked lots of people about their fears and insecurities. The most common answers were job interviews, doctor/dentist appointments, meetings, parties and large social gatherings. Do you know what your fears and insecurities are? The exercise below may help you to identify them.

Exercise: My Fears and Insecurities

It might seem hard to believe but every single one of us has fears and insecurities. Some wear them like a battle scar, while others conceal them. You've heard the expression 'fake it till it becomes real'. If that's what it takes then do it.

Give yourself permission to have fears and insecurities sometimes; just don't allow them to rule your life.

You will need a piece of paper and a pen for this exercise.

1. Write a list of your fears and insecurities. Your list should include all those situations and relationships that you find difficult

2. Once your list is complete prioritise the items; one being the most important

3. You can't deal with all your issues at once so start with your number one issue. See, feel and experience this issue as clearly as possible

4. Give yourself permission to feel fearful or insecure for a short while. Allow yourself 1-24 hours for this part of the exercise. This is your self-pity or woe is me time

5. When the time is up, it's time to tackle the issue. Make a commitment to yourself that you're going to beat this fear

6. Identify if this fear is rational or irrational

7. Now decide how you're going to deal with this. If your fear is rational then it has the potential to harm you in some way. Decide what practical actions you can do to prevent or overcome this fear

8. If your fear is irrational this may be easier to deal with. You could do something physical e.g. go for a run, Zumba, dance or go for a walk etc. You may prefer meditation or mood boards. Some people like to read positive affirmations, while others like to talk to a friend. There is no right or wrong way to tackle your irrational fears and insecurities

9. Obviously the action you take matters to a degree. However, the most important thing is to do something. This tells your brain you're doing something positive to deal with your confidence issues

10. When this fear no longer has a stranglehold over you, reward your bravery in some way

11. When you feel ready, tackle the next fear on your list. Never try to deal with more than one issue at a time as you'll end up putting yourself under unnecessary pressure

Fear isn't always a bad thing. Sometimes fear sharpens your awareness, which may help you avoid potentially harmful situations. This form of fear is your in-built protection system.

A bit of anxiety (irrational fear) can get your adrenalin running. This encourages you to perform better in certain situations. For example, adrenalin can help you rise to the challenge of a job interview. Adrenalin is also helpful if you have to deliver a presentation or do some public speaking.

Rational fear is a survival instinct and a knee jerk reaction. It's the fight or flight decision you make. This decision is made in a split second and doesn't give you time for reasoning or logical thought.

Irrational fear can be a confidence breaker and a great inhibitor to achieving your goals and aspirations. Like confidence, fear is triggered by what you think, say and do. The more you concentrate on fear the more scared you will become.

When fear kicks in it's the ideal time to practice deep breathing or mindfulness unless the situation is serious or life threatening. Deep breathing or mindfulness will give you the chance to calm down and make a logical decision. Even a couple of minutes can make a difference to your decision making.

Irrational fear feels real, so the challenge is learning how to deal with it. Confident people find a way to experience the fear and then swiftly move on. This is the key to success. Trying to never feel fear simply won't work.

If you're unsure whether your fears are rational or irrational, perhaps this will help:

Here is an example of rational fear. You're walking home after dark and consider using a short-cut down an alley. Your survival instinct kicks in and tells you this isn't a good idea. This fear is good as your emotional state is trying to protect you from potential harm.

Now to an example of irrational fear... A common irrational fear is public speaking or delivering a workplace presentation. Do you feel paralysed at the mere thought of public speaking or delivering a presentation to your colleagues?

The logical part of your brain will be saying "this isn't going to kill me". Your emotional state still feels the fear anyway. The reason for this fear is you're imagining it going badly, rather than imagining it being successful.

In this case, you need to reprogramme your brain to expect success. The end result will then be increased self-confidence. This confidence will then give you the courage to tackle the task.

Don't let your irrational fear of failure hold you back. Of course you will have failures in life - we all do. Failure contributes to how we learn and grow. Remember, you didn't come out of your mother's womb walking and talking. You overcame many setbacks before you achieved both of these goals, and many others.

Fear of success is also an irrational fear. Some people are actually more scared of success than failure. I'm not a psychologist so I'm not the best person to explain the reason for this. However, I do believe that it's just as important to overcome this fear as any other fear. Any kind of fear has the potential to harm or restrict your self-confidence.

Susanne Babbel Ph.D. MFT featured an exercise in Psychology Today (3 January 2011) for developing a healthy relationship with success. Here is the exercise she suggested:

1. Recall an event where you were successful or excited when you were younger, and notice what you are feeling and sensing in your memory. Stay with the sensation of success for 5 minutes

2. Recall an event where you were successful and excited recently in your life, and notice what you are feeling and sensing. Stay with this sensation of success for 5 minutes

3. Now tap into the sensation of a memory of an overwhelming situation. I suggest not starting with a truly traumatic event, at least not without a therapist's support. Start with something only moderately disturbing to you

4. Now, go back to visualising your success story. Do you notice a difference?

Learn to recognise and challenge your irrational fears when they occur. Don't allow your negative thoughts a free rein as this can lead to a lack of self-confidence. Whenever you have a negative thought consciously replace it with a positive one. With practice this will become second nature.

Confident people don't ignore fear but they understand when it's rational and when it's irrational. They know irrational fear gets in the way of what they want to achieve. Therefore, they deal with it and move forward. Try it and see how you get on.

Exercise: Tackling My Irrational Fears

At some point in our lives we will all be faced with an irrational fear. That's just part of what makes us human. Here's your chance to deal with one of your irrational fears.

You will need a piece of paper and a pen for this exercise.

1. Think of one of your 'fear situations'. For example, a job interview, delivering a presentation, taking an exam, getting married etc

2. Identify whether this fear is rational or irrational. Be honest with yourself. If your fear is irrational don't try to justify it as this won't solve the problem. Just acknowledge it for now

3. Allow yourself to experience your fear as if it's happening now. You may need to remind yourself that you're practicing this is a safe environment

4. Now do a positive mental visualisation of the same situation. See yourself handling the situation confidently. Keep doing this until your new positive mental attitude feels real. It may take several attempts to change your thinking but keep trying

5. You've now successfully got this irrational fear into perspective. Know that it no longer holds any power over you. You may always feel uncomfortable giving a presentation but you will learn to manage your anxiety. Channel your anxiety to give you an adrenalin boost

Next time you're faced with a situation that you fear try this exercise. Notice what you're thinking. The more vividly you see and feel the fear the more real it will seem to you. Then use a positive visualisation to manage that fear.

You can use this exercise as an antidote for any irrational fear situation. It won't always remove the fear completely, but it will certainly contribute to neutralising your irrational fears. The more you can control your fears the more your self-confidence will be able to develop and grow.

Is one of your irrational fears meeting new people? This is a very common fear. Although you may feel uncomfortable or tongue-tied, meeting new people is not life threatening. This is why it's an irrational fear.

There are steps you can take to overcome this fear. This doesn't mean you will automatically enjoy meeting new people. However, you will be able to deal with the situation more confidently in future.

Start by visualising how you currently feel when you meet new people for the first time. Make your visual image as clear as possible; the clearer your images the better the result.

Once you have a clear image in your mind, acknowledge your fear, and the harm this is doing to your self-confidence. Now ask yourself what you are scared of. Typical answers include being rebuffed or the person not wanting to speak to you. Make a mental note of what your fears are.

Next, imagine that the person does ignore you. Ask yourself "is this someone I really want to be friendly with?" Why would you want to be friendly with someone who has no regard for you? That would simply be an act of self-sabotage.

The next question to ask yourself is "does this person's opinion matter to me?" If so, why does this person's opinion matter? If his/her opinion doesn't matter you've already overcome your fear.

Of course, usually people will respond positively. Remember, others may be experiencing the same fears as you. No one wanders around with a sandwich board around their neck stating "I fear being ignored".

Next time you meet someone new test the water and see how they react to you. You will probably never know how anxious or relaxed the other person feels. Rest assured some people will be grateful that you made the first move.

Start by smiling at the other person. If the person doesn't respond, move onto someone else. If he/she responds to your smile try starting the conversation with a safe subject. For example, who do you know at the party? What brought you to this event today? I haven't seen you in the office before. Have you worked for the company for long?

After you have done this, spend a few minutes reflecting on how you feel now. Hopefully it will have given you a tiny confidence boost. Remember, lots of small steps add up to great big leaps of self-confidence.

So, how do you feel about change and fear now? Whether you look forward to change or dread it, change triggers powerful effects on your body and emotions. Not all change is good, but most change contains elements of good.

If you know how to view life positively you will be better equipped to deal with change. Here are seven tips on how to deal with change. I hope these will be useful on your journey to increased self-confidence.

- Accept that you're in the midst of change and that change is a part of you. This might seem like a no-brainer, but it takes practice to become aware of change instead of subconsciously denying it. Don't run and hide from change as it will find you anyway

- Face your fears about the change, especially when the change is beyond your control. Get past "Why me?" "But I don't want to..." and "It isn't fair". Identify what your fears and worries are. You don't have to be a victim, even when you're not in control of the change

- Decide when to accept and when to reject the change. Change for changes sake is often a waste of time and energy. If there's a reason for the change it's much easier to accept it

- Adopt an attitude of anticipation and gratitude. View change as an opportunity, not a threat. There is always a benefit and an opportunity, no matter how small. Challenge yourself to find it. Start by keeping a written record for three days. At the end of each day make a note of three things from today that you feel grateful for

- Be aware that you choose your thoughts and attitudes about change. Negative thoughts block your creativity and problem solving abilities. Positive thoughts build bridges to possibilities and opportunities

- Learn to relax more. Some people find exercise or physical activity helps them relax. Others find meditation or deep breathing works best. Find what works for you. Relaxation enables you to deal with change better

- Use change to your advantage and make it one of your strategies for increasing your self-confidence. Remember, every change increases your skills, knowledge or experience toolkit

The only other thing to say about change, fear and self-confidence is communicate with supportive people who can help you. These people will help you embrace change and minimise the stress often associated with change.

"Change might be challenging but it won't kill you. Every change is an opportunity to grow and develop. As you grow, so will your self-confidence" - Elizabeth J Tucker

9. Conclusion

"Everything worth doing lies on the other side of fear" - Georgina Gould

Together we've been on quite a long journey since you did the 'Crisis of Confidence' exercise in chapter 1. So, how are you feeling now? Do you know yourself better now? Perhaps more importantly, do you know how you developed low self-confidence, and have you dealt with any of your issues?

In 'A Matter of Self-confidence - Part I' we've looked at your reasons for lack of self-confidence. You've had an opportunity to consider your ego, lack of self-confidence traits, and your personal beliefs. Probably the biggie was looking at your fears and attitude to change.

I hope 'A Matter of Self-confidence - Part I' has helped you to identify where your issues stem from. Now it's time to take action. 'A Matter of Self-confidence - Part II' will hold your hand as you begin to create a more confident future.

Are you a great procrastinator, or are you ready to take a leap of faith? Remember, all talk but no action results in no change. Here's a riddle for you to consider...

Twelve frogs are sitting on their own lily pad in the pond in the garden. Five of the frogs decide to jump into the water. How many frogs are left sitting on their lily pad?

In case you haven't spotted the correct answer - it's twelve. While five frogs decided to jump into the water the riddle doesn't say they did it. That's procrastination for you.

"Procrastination is often linked to low self-confidence. It's due to fear of putting your reputation on the line. Face your fears" - Elizabeth J Tucker

If you've identified what needs to happen to overcome your self-confidence issues pat yourself on the back. You've taken a big step towards greater self-confidence.

Don't stop now. The next step of your self-confidence journey is taking action. Your self-confidence is the result of the action you take, not your thoughts. Developing sustainable self-confidence will require having the courage to step outside your comfort zone. I know you can succeed.

Before you make any decisions about where you go from here, why not reflect on your journey so far. Make a list of five things you've learnt or have achieved as a result of reading 'A Matter of Self-confidence - Part I'.

1.

2.

3.

4.

5.

The purpose of 'A Matter of Self-confidence' is to help you overcome your fears and acquire new confidence. Building self-confidence is a marathon, not a sprint, but here are some quick fixes that will give you an instant boost.

Physical appearance: Yes, physical appearance does have a part to play in developing your self-confidence. No one is more conscious of your physical appearance than you are. Feeling good in what you're wearing makes you present yourself differently.

You don't need to spend a fortune on the clothes you wear but always buy the best you can afford as it will make you feel good.

Posture: Good posture has a role to play in giving the impression of confidence. Make eye contact, straighten your spine, put your shoulders back and hold your head up. You will feel more energised, but also you will immediately give the impression of greater self-confidence. This will empower you and draw others to you as self-confidence works like a magnet.

If your shoulders are slumped and your head is down you give the impression of lack of self-confidence or lack of interest. You convey the same message if you appear lethargic. Both have the same result - people won't rush to be with you.

Put a pep in your step: I know this sounds a bit clichéd. Be energetic and purposeful when you walk. This sends out a message of self-confidence. If your walking is slow, tired and laboured you send the opposite message. Give the impression that you've got places to go and things to do.

Physical activity: I'm not suggesting that you rush off and join a gym (unless that's something you want to do). Any increase in physical activity will help your self-confidence. This could be as simple as getting off the bus one stop earlier. If you feel physically well you will have a more positive body image. This will help you to appear more confident.

Move to the front row: Are you one of those people who always sit at the back in conferences and presentations? People who lack self-confidence often prefer to sit in the back and hope they won't be noticed. Force yourself out of your comfort zone and sit in the front row instead. This will help you overcome your fear of being noticed, which in turn will build your self-confidence.

Motivational speakers: Listening to motivational speakers can be very uplifting as they exude self-confidence. Remember, some of them make a fortune out of motivational speaking, so they must be doing something right.

Listen to what they have to say and adopt some of their habits. If you can't afford to attend seminars and lectures download motivational speeches. Writing and reciting your own 60 second elevator pitch is a great way to boost your self-confidence.

Find your voice: If you're one of those people who never, or rarely, contributes in meetings; it's time to find your voice. The chances are you have a valuable contribution to make, but hiding your light under a bushel isn't helpful. Speaking up might take you out of your comfort zone initially, but afterwards you will feel so much more confident.

If it helps, other people at the meeting probably have the same fears as you. However, they push themselves forward as they understand how important it is. You will never get a promotion if the organisation doesn't know what you have to offer.

Think and speak positively: People who lack self-confidence often talk negatively about other people as well as themselves. This negative habit can turn into a downward spiral.

Challenge yourself to find something positive to say about yourself and everyone you meet for a day. At the end of the day reflect on how much better you feel. Also try using positive affirmations to develop your self-confidence.

Stop being selfish: People who lack self-confidence often become self-absorbed by constantly feeling sorry for themselves. Confident people tend not to be so self-absorbed.

Confident people are more likely to focus on the contribution they're making to the world, and the needs of others. The more you contribute to the world around you the more personal success and recognition you will achieve. This is turn will do wonders for your self-confidence.

Gratitude: Being grateful is one of the best ways to develop a positive outlook. Start by being grateful for your strengths, skills and all the material things you have in your life. This will help you realise how much you've got going for you. Gratitude and positive thinking are great for increasing self-confidence.

The more grateful you are the more good things will come your way. As your life gets better you'll feel so much happier and more confident.

I hope 'A Matter of Self-confidence - Part I' has helped you in some small way. The aim of this book was to help you understand how you arrived at your current lack of self-confidence. 'A Matter of Self-Confidence - Part II' focuses on creating the confident future you want and deserve.

You owe it to yourself to develop self-confidence. Remember confidence translates as:

C - Communication is fundamental to effective contact with others. Communicate your thoughts, feelings and needs

O - Open yourself up to the opportunities, ideas and new experiences available to you. Who knows where it may take you

N - Negotiate what you want and need. Stop believing other people's needs take priority

F - Fight for your rights and face up to the consequences of your self-limiting beliefs. Stop blaming others for anything that's wrong in your life

I - Influence others to your way of thinking instead of trying to control them. There's a subtle difference

D - Dare to believe in yourself. This will do wonders for your self-confidence

E - Expect the best possible outcomes. Of course things won't always work out this way, but you'll have the confidence to deal with whatever happens

N - Nurture yourself. You're worth it!

C - Change what you can and learn to graciously accept what you can't change

E - Enjoy your journey to increased self-confidence. I guarantee you won't want to go back to your old ways

One single strategy or action won't instantly increase your self-confidence. However, all the little steps you take towards this goal will pay dividends. Good luck and happy confidence building!

"Doing your own thing requires self-confidence and determination but the rewards are worth the effort. Don't let self-doubt hold you back" - Elizabeth J Tucker

10. Appendices

In the Appendices section I have included some common terms used when discussing self-confidence. After the terms and definitions you will find the answers to the Reality or Myth Quiz. In this section I've also included some affirmations to get you started and a self-confidence progress log.

Terms and Definitions

There are lots of terms used when discussing self-confidence. I thought you might find it helpful to have a list of the most commonly used terms and their definition:

Arrogance - this involves believing you're better at something than you are. For arrogant people being right is more important than being capable

Ego - the dictionary defines this as the opinion that you have about yourself. According to Freud your ego prevents you from acting on your basic urges, but also works to achieve a balance with your moral and idealistic standards

Low self-esteem - this involves believing you're less valuable than you are

Morale - is about your feelings of enthusiasm and loyalty regarding a task or job. Morale is sometimes used for describing groups as well as individuals

Narcissism - this is about craving admiration from others. This is also often demonstrated by extreme selfishness and lack of empathy with others

Overconfidence - this may be a front for lack of self-confidence. Overconfidence often appears to others as arrogance or cockiness. Scratch the surface and find out what lies beneath

Self-assurance - is confidence in the validity and value of your own ideas and opinions

Self-centred - much like narcissism, this is limited to caring only about yourself and your own needs

Self-confidence - this involves knowing what you're good at and the value you provide. This is not arrogance as you have a healthy and honest opinion of what you're good at and what you're not good at

Self-esteem - in psychology, the term self-esteem is used to describe your overall sense of self-worth or personal value. Self-esteem can involve a variety of beliefs about yourself, such as your appearance, beliefs, emotions, and behaviours

Self-possession - this describes your control over your emotions or reactions, especially when under stress

Self-regard - the dictionary describes this as the quality of being worthy of esteem or respect

Self-respect - this means respecting yourself above all else. If you don't respect yourself it's unlikely that you will receive respect from other people

Self-worth - the dictionary defines self-worth as "the sense of one's own value or worth as a person"

The Dunning-Kruger effect - this is where unskilled individuals suffer from illusory superiority. As you're reading this book I suspect this is not an issue for you

Vanity - this is the excessive belief in your own abilities or attractiveness to others

If you answered the Reality or Myth Quiz at the start of the book, here are the answers:

Exercise: Reality or Myth Quiz Answers

1. We are all born confident - Reality/Myth
Answer: Reality and myth. When we're born we have no experiences other than the birthing process. This is probably one of the few times in life when we accept 'just being'. Through our life experiences our self-confidence grows or disappears

2. I had a difficult or emotionally barren childhood. As a result of this I will never be confident - Reality/Myth
Answer: Myth. Although a traumatic childhood may make it more difficult to develop self-confidence, it's your choice. The future doesn't have to mirror the past. Everyone can develop self-confidence, but first you have to want to do it

3. I know I lack self-confidence as I'm nervous in social situations - Reality/Myth
Answer: Myth. You may feel uncomfortable or lack self-confidence in social situations. This doesn't automatically mean that you lack self-confidence in every area of your life. You can work on this area of your life and overcome your anxieties

4. I lack self-confidence as I'm not as attractive or smart as the other people in my network - Reality/Myth
Answer: Myth. Self-confidence has nothing to do with looks or ability. It's about your internal belief system. Even the most beautiful people can, and do, lack self-confidence

5. Other people keep putting me down, and so I lack self-confidence - Reality/Myth
Answer: Myth. Other people's comments may be unkind and unnecessary, but they don't cause the pain. The problem is you care too much about what other people think, and not enough about what you think. You choose to accept these comments as your reality

6. Low self-esteem causes fear - Reality/Myth
Answer: Myth. Low self-esteem is caused by fear, not the other way around. This can be fear of failure, fear of success or just fear of any kind of change

7. People with high self-esteem are arrogant - Reality/Myth
Answer: Myth. Arrogance is an inflated opinion of self-worth or superiority. Self-esteem is about being satisfied with who you are and recognising what you have to offer

8. Everyone can develop self-confidence - Reality/Myth
Answer: Reality. Self-confidence is like any other skill. With commitment, practice and effort anyone can develop self-confidence

9. Highly self-confident people also have fears, anxieties and lack of self-confidence sometimes - Reality/Myth
Answer: Reality. Confident people learn to manage their fears and anxieties so insecurity doesn't govern their life

10. Lack of self-confidence comes from our insecurities - Reality/Myth
Answer: Reality. If you can get your insecurities under control lack of self-confidence won't rule your life

11. Arrogance and self-confidence is the same thing - Reality/Myth
Answer: Myth. Having self-confidence is a wonderful asset that will help you to successfully navigate life. Arrogance is rooted in insecurity. An arrogant person generally has a skewed view of the world and a warped understanding of themselves. They often build themselves up by putting others down, to 'win'

Exercise: Affirmations

Affirmations are short powerful statements. Like mantras, affirmations have a role to play in all aspects of your life. One of the great things about affirmations is you can use them wherever and whenever you wish.

1. Why not challenge yourself to create your own personal set of affirmations. These are the personal messages that will help build your self-confidence. Here are some affirmations to get you started:

- I'm amazing as I am
- I'm becoming more confident by caring for myself and learning strategies to grow my self-confidence
- I'm proud of all my achievements - big and small
- I'm special with every single cell in my body
- I'm surrounded by very lovely and genuine friends who only wish the best for me. For my part - I'm a good friend too
- I'm unique
- I'm what I am and that's ok
- I can do anything that I set my mind to do
- I feel positive energy running through my entire body
- If I truly want something I will achieve it
- I have released my fears and now accept that as I successfully overcome my challenges so my self-confidence grows
- I have the self-confidence to achieve whatever I want to achieve. I recognise that my world is only limited by my own imagination
- I just get better and more confident every day. I use my new self-confidence to help others who are less confident than me
- I like myself as I am
- I'm a beautiful confident human being, who embraces my strengths and weaknesses equally
- I'm confident in my abilities
- I'm great as I am and don't need to change to please others
- I no longer need to feel anxious as I know I'm good enough as I am
- I will put all my strength into my actions, and I will break any obstacle that may rise
- There is no-one and nothing that can stop me achieving my goals. I am the best I can be

2. Repeat your affirmation (positive message) in your head as often as you wish. You should do this several times a day, every day until you truly believe the messages you're saying or thinking. This is brain training, not brain washing

Exercise: My Self-confidence Progress Log

Identifying when your confidence grows is an essential part of speeding up the process of increased self-confidence. The more aware you become of your growing self-confidence the more confident you will become, and so the cycle continues.

1. Before you start your self-confidence journey it's important to identify your current confidence level. Otherwise it will be impossible for you to notice how well you're doing.

At the end of the exercise instructions you will find a 12 week chart, which will enable you to plot your progress.

2. When you're ready put a cross in the relevant box on the 'Before' line. This is your self-confidence level before you begin working to increase it. For example - you might feel you current confidence level is 4

3. Each week spend a few minutes reflecting on how you feel. Notice how you feel about yourself, your skills and your self-confidence. Put a cross in the relevant box for that week

4. At the end of week 12 look at your chart and notice the progress you've made. Even the smallest increase in self-confidence is a big step forward

5. Don't forget to reward your success at the end of week 12 as this will help to keep you motivated. It also tells your brain that you're doing something positive

	0 (low)	1	2	3	4	5	6	7	8	9	10
Week 12											
Week 11											
Week 10											
Week 9											
Week 8											
Week 7											
Week 6											
Week 5											
Week 4											
Week 3											
Week 2											
Week 1											
Before											
	0 (low)	1	2	3	4	5	6	7	8	9	10

Success starts with self-confidence!

Lightning Source UK Ltd.
Milton Keynes UK
UKOW06f0207231117
313184UK00007B/167/P

9 780993 114519